Can leading be ea

Church leadership does
for burnout. There is an easier way, one that
is doable, effective, and sustainable. It is
counterintuitive, though, so help is needed to
get it right. This book will give you that help.
Learn how you can:

- Be more of a leader and less of a controller.
- Adopt a new system of seeing yourself and those you lead.
- Focus on yourself and the resources you bring rather than trying to help, fix, or change others.
- Respond to others with more clarity, calm, and creativity.
- Remain more thoughtful during challenge and crisis.
- Increase your influence without increasing your workload.
- Reduce your overall stress about issues of congregational life.

The Reverend Margaret Marcuson speaks and writes
on leadership and works with church leaders nationally
as a consultant and coach. She is a frequent guest
preacher in churches, and her conference speaking and
consulting crosses denominations. Margaret served
as pastor of the First Baptist Church of Gardner,
Massachusetts, for thirteen years. Since 1999, she has
taught in the Leadership in Ministry workshops, a clergy
leadership training program. Margaret is the author of
111 Tips to Survive Pastoral Ministry. She is a graduate
of the Pacific School of Religion, and was a student
of Edwin Friedman. She lives in Portland, Oregon.

Find out more at www.margaretmarcuson.com.

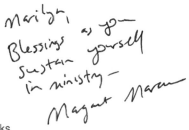

LEADERS
WHO LAST

SUSTAINING YOURSELF
AND YOUR MINISTRY

MARGARET J. MARCUSON

Marilyn,
Blessings as you
sustain yourself
in ministry —
Margaret Marcu

 Seabury Books

An imprint of Church Publishing Incorporated, New York

Library of Congress Cataloging-in-Publication Data
Marcuson, Margaret J.
Leaders who last : sustaining yourself and your ministry /
Margaret J. Marcuson.
    p.   cm.
Includes bibliographical references.
ISBN 978-1-59627-095-4 (pbk.)
1. Christian leadership. I. Title.
BV652.1.M359 2009
253—dc22

                                        2008048506

Cover design by Brenda Klinger
Interior design by Vicki K. Black

Printed in the United States of America.

Seabury Books
445 Fifth Avenue
New York, New York 10016
www.seaburybooks.com
An imprint of Church Publishing Incorporated

5   4   3   2   1

CONTENTS

ACKNOWLEDGMENTS

This book would not exist without Edwin Friedman, who changed my thinking about my approach to pastoral leadership and to life in general. I am eternally grateful.

I am also thankful to Larry Matthews, for his commitment to helping clergy be better leaders, especially by encouraging them to face the challenges of their own families of origin and how their own story affects their functioning in ministry. I have received at least as much as I have given while teaching in Larry's Leadership in Ministry workshop.

My editor, Cynthia Shattuck, has helped me become a better writer and made this a better book. I am in awe of her skill. Others who have helped me with the writing process include Jill Kelly and the writing group she facilitates, and my friend and colleague Meg Hess, who helped keep my feet to the fire with our "shut up and write" dates.

The following people read and commented on chapters: Jim Boyer, Paul Brassey, Larry Foster, Israel Galindo, Kent Harrop, David Hutchinson, Marianne LaBarre, James Lamkin, John Rosenberg, Rob Schachter, Brad Shumate, Gregg Sneller, Jody Stevenson, and Jeff Woods. Ken Arnold helped me immeasurably as I learned about the publishing process.

My family was very patient with me, and my daughter Hannah helped edit a number of chapters. My husband Karl has always been my biggest fan, and I am thankful. My parents, brother, and son all read the chapter about our family and are still speaking to me.

I am grateful to those many generations who have gone before, both in family and church, who have influenced what I have become, and so these words.

*This book is dedicated
to my parents and grandparents.*

CHAPTER 1

LASTING LEADERSHIP:

IS IT POSSIBLE?

One Easter Sunday I was standing in the back of the church I served, waiting for the service to start. The place was packed; the prelude music was soaring. The choir and I were ready to process down the aisle, and I could hardly wait for Easter worship to begin. Then I felt a tap on my shoulder, and I looked over and saw a member of the executive board. He leaned over and said in my ear, "You know, I think we're going to have to do something about that cracked toilet."

I wanted to shout at him, "Why are you telling me this now?" I thought, how can I lead these people toward spiritual maturity when all they care about is the cracked toilet? I kept reflecting on this apparent fact in the weeks to come and the experience catapulted me into a crisis in my ministry. I seriously thought about leaving the church and doing something else. I felt like I was pushing the people in the church uphill, to make them become what I thought they should be—a vital, spiritually focused and growing church—and I was exhausted. Ultimately, though, I found a way to stay engaged and to revitalize my ministry—and I stayed at that congregation for nine more years.

I came close to burning out in ministry, just as many clergy do: some leave ministry altogether, while others experience periods of burnout without leaving. Some simply feel discouraged, and find it hard to function effectively. The author of the second letter to Timothy wrote, "I have fought the good fight, I have finished the race, I have kept the faith. From now on there is reserved for me the crown of righteousness, which the Lord, the righteous judge, will give me on that day" (2 Timothy 4:7–8). Will we all be able to say this at the conclusion of our ministry? You may hear these words—"I have fought the good fight, I have finished the race, I have kept the faith"—and think, "How?" You may wonder how to keep going when you are exhausted, when moving the congregation forward even an inch seems so difficult, when you are not sure what finishing the race would look like.

Our society is anxious and so are the Christian congregations within it. We may feel our actual survival is at stake, and we struggle to think creatively about ministry in this new context. We, and everyone else, are looking for a quick fix: a new strategy, program, or technique that will help us out of the morass where we find ourselves.

Denominational life can seem like one conflict after another. The Reverend Kate Harvey, executive director of the American Baptist Churches Ministers Council, puts it this way: "I have long observed the cross-fire tendency of our age, with cohorts at opposite ends of the spectrum of perspective on an issue choosing to polarize and mirror image the very behavior they claim to detest. . . . It takes considerable work to resist being drawn into that place."

We church leaders place high expectations on ourselves, adding even more pressure internally. We judge our value by how the ministry is going. I can remember as a pastor sitting in church on Sunday and looking out at the congregation. My mood that day depended on whether attendance was up or down that week. I gauged my own success by the numbers. Is it possible to last and even thrive as a leader? The author of 2 Timothy says yes, but to find the same endurance, we have to know what is meant by "the good fight." We have to know what race we are running, and what it means to keep the faith.

"*I have fought the good fight.*" We can get caught in wars of words if not fists, just as the apostles faced their share of conflict. What if, in fact, the good fight does not mean conflict, but effort? We then would need to consider where we want to spend our limited life energy, how it would be most fruitful, and what we would want our legacy to be when we look back.

"*I have finished the race.*" We can spend a lot of time running in place, or running in someone else's race. Many people—both external experts and our followers—want to tell us which race we should run. Discerning the right race for us is the task of the leader.

"*I have kept the faith.*" There is rarely an easy fix in ministry and in life. Most things of value take time to grow. A slow fix lasts longer than a quick fix, but it requires a long-term view we and others do not always have. When we keep the faith, we have patience with ourselves and with others. Most of us have personal challenges that we will work on for a lifetime. When we keep the faith, we keep working on ourselves. Most congregations have issues of one kind or another that will never completely go away. When we keep the faith, we persistently call people to gentle account and offer them the opportunity slowly to move forward.

☙ MANAGING OURSELVES

Here is the heart of what it takes to sustain leadership. We move from the impossible—controlling others—to the merely difficult—managing ourselves. When I hear leaders begin with a question like, "How can I get them to...?" then I know that different questions need to be asked: "What is my part in the problem? How can I clarify what I think about this issue? How can I clearly communicate my own point of view?" We *can* in fact manage ourselves, if we choose to. We cannot control others. But we can offer our point of view, challenge them, and give them room to respond.

When I was leading a church, I found this reality liberating. For example, in my preaching I was responsible to do my best to preach God's word as I understood it to that community, and to challenge them to be and do more. But they were responsible before God for what they did with that word. It took the pressure off, and I felt relieved. I knew preaching was still vital. But I reframed it as a task I could do, rather than one I had been trying so hard to do that it was not working. The question changed from "How can I get them to hear?" to "What am I called to say to them this week?" I found my preaching was reenergized, and noticed people responding in new ways.

When we understand more deeply both ourselves and our relationships with others, we are less likely to be blindsided by opposition to ideas we think are terrific. We will not get worn out trying to get other people to do what we want. We will avoid the exhausting role of constantly cajoling, cheerleading, and pushing people in the direction we want to go. We will know what we need to keep going.

Lasting as a leader does not mean finding an easy way to do it: there is no easy way. We will always face setbacks and discouragements, and at times we will throw up our hands in despair. But as we persevere, we will also find times for satisfaction and celebration.

First of all, we must begin to know who we are, and our unique calling from God. Discerning our identity and call is not a matter for a moment, but for a lifetime. Second, we need to understand the complexities of what happens in relationships between people, whether in families, churches, or wider society. Likewise, this study is a lifetime process.

If we do not understand ourselves, our giftedness as well as our own vulnerabilities, we will find it hard to last in ministry. And when we do become clear on who we are and what we are to do, the task of leadership does not become easy, but it does become easier. I am an amateur singer, and my voice teacher tells me that when I try to sing like someone else, it sounds bad. Trying too hard to sing in a way I was not made to sing damages the voice. She says I am a coloratura soprano, which means I do not have a huge voice. Certain songs I was not meant to sing, and other songs I have to sing in a way that is not forced or too loud. But when I can open my mouth and let it out, it can be beautiful, and gives me and others a lot of pleasure.

We also need to learn how to develop the emotional and spiritual muscles that will sustain us. Soprano Renée Fleming says in *The Inner Voice: The Making of a Singer,* "When a singer uses her body and breath properly to support the voice, it takes the strain completely off the throat." While others may help support us in our leadership role, we cannot substitute anything else for internal support. When we develop this support, we come through with less strain, and with more energy and hope.

We cannot lead others further than we are willing to go ourselves. If we want people to go deeper in the spiritual life, if we want them to grow up emotionally, if we want them to be more authentic, we have to show the way. Leadership starts with us. In a way our own life is familiar, but we do not always know the unseen forces that are driving us. Mastering our own territory, knowing who we are, is a lifetime's work. Jesus said, "First take the log out of your own eye, and then you will see clearly to take the speck out of your neighbor's eye" (Matthew 7:5).

Father Paul Schroeder of Holy Trinity Greek Orthodox Cathedral in Portland, Oregon, tells this story from his time at Holy Cross Seminary. "On a trip to Mount Athos, at one of the monasteries there was a young monk who had formerly been a fellow student at Holy Cross. We visited his monastery, and had an opportunity to speak with him privately. At one point, one of my classmates named George asked him, in a mock serious tone, 'So, have you found peace here?' Without a moment's hesitation, the young monk leaned over and touched my friend on the chest and said, 'George, peace is in your heart. If you don't find it there, you won't find it anywhere else.'" Pastoral ministry is not the place to look for peace of mind. It can be satisfying, inspiring, and gratifying at times. But the peace of mind we receive from ministry will be the peace of mind we bring to it. We need a sense of self apart from the response we receive. When we are less dependent on the approval of others, we can be more effective in our ministry.

☙ LEARNING THE TERRITORY
In addition to knowing the territory of our own lives, we also have to know the lay of the land we are traveling. Families, congregations, and denominations are systems that add up to more than the individuals involved. Patterns develop in these systems that persist over time. We often think it will be easy to change those patterns, but it is better to realize the power of the system, which often is more powerful than any one leader. Systems need leaders, but we cannot snap our fingers and expect everything to change quickly because our new vision makes sense to us. When we expect quick change, we are bound to be frustrated. Simply knowing that leadership is long-term will help us keep the faith.

Of course, the power of the system is not all bad: systems have great resilience and the ability to maintain themselves, which can serve us well. Learning how balance is maintained in systems, how people create triangles, and how ways of relating are passed down through the generations will help us sustain our leadership with less frustration and more clarity.

What is the territory of your particular congregation or ministry setting? What is its history, its skeletons and secrets, its past triumphs and present strengths? What will happen when you take a stand on this particular issue, or chart a course in that direction? Do you know your people well enough? And are you open to being surprised by them?

Leadership in ministry involves the spiritual practice of paying attention: to God, to ourselves, to those we lead, and the environment we lead within. This is a full-time job. It is rarely an easy job. In his essay "Genesis," Wallace Stegner describes a young green cowhand, Rusty, taking part in a cattle drive. A blizzard overtakes them before they reach their destination, and they barely survive. When they reach shelter and are recovering, as Rusty is soaking his frostbitten feet, one of the other men, Little Horn, says, "There's no business like the cow business to make a man healthy and active. There's hardly a job you can work at that'll keep you more in the open air."

Rusty thinks to himself, as he reflects on his experience, "What would pass for heroics in a softer world was only chores around here."[1] Physical survival may not be at stake in our ministry, but at times everything else in our lives—emotional, financial, and spiritual—can seem to be. We take one plodding step at a time, and wonder when we will emerge from the blizzard into someplace clear, bright, and warm.

Perseverance is one of the chores of leadership. We do our best to keep going. Sometimes we can see the big picture, and that vision energizes us (and others in turn). Other times, in the big storms that are part of the territory of leadership, we do not know exactly how things will turn out. Often the only way out is to go *through* it, to move ahead through the storm.

And at the same time, with Little Horn, we can acknowledge that "there's no business like leadership." Nothing else puts us on the line in quite the same way; nothing else stretches us, helps us grow as leaders and as human beings. Some days we may want to look for a way out. We may roll our eyes and say, "Why me?" or, "Not again!" Instead, we might take a deep breath and embrace the challenge. Leadership can be invigorating rather than simply exhausting.

❧ WHAT TO EXPECT

In this book you can expect to find ways to become more thoughtful about the challenges you face in your ministry, and to respond with more clarity, calm, and creativity as you move forward. The approach to leadership you will see here is founded in psychiatrist Murray Bowen's family systems theory, especially as articulated by therapist and rabbi Edwin Friedman, who applied family systems thinking to congregational life. You can expect to learn basic systems ideas and how they apply to ministry, and to find ways to think about ministry dilemmas and how to approach them.

In addition to foundational concepts, you will meet real-life leaders from around the country and across denominations who have sought to put these ideas into practice in their own leadership. You will also find practical tips and questions to help you think through the purpose and direction of your own ministry, and how to handle yourself in the middle of ministry challenges.

When leaders can combine a clear sense of themselves and their God-given purpose with a wise understanding of human relationships, ministry can prosper. Acting on what you learn in this book will enhance your understanding both of yourself and of those you lead, making the work of leadership easier. Being a church leader is never easy, but it is easier when you focus on what you can control: yourself and your response to others. This book addresses the heart of what you have to offer in leadership: your unique gifts, clarity, and the ability to make connections with those you lead.

The early followers of Jesus knew about disgruntled church members, factions within congregations, and money struggles, just as we do. They knew about messages that were misinterpreted, becoming the focus of everyone's discontent, and the challenges of pioneering a new way of being church. Still, at the end, the author of the second letter to Timothy shares a word of completion: "I have fought the good fight, I have finished the race, I have kept the faith." He had done his part, and others he had nurtured were carrying on. May we, like him, at the end, experience a sense of satisfaction with our work in response to God's call.

CHAPTER 2

TAKE RESPONSIBILITY
FOR YOURSELF

I just don't know what to do, Pastor." She sat in my office, pouring out her heart to me about her difficulties with her son. I wished I could reach into that family and rearrange things. I would make her son get a job and move out, if I could. I sat across from her, struggling with my anxiety and sense of inadequacy.

What does it mean to be truly helpful in ministry? Most clergy feel a sense of calling to make a difference for others in the world. We want to engage with others, support them through crises, and help them grow. Yet our efforts at helping may not lead to growth, but to dependency. We can cause people to lean on us more than on their own resources. We can have trouble understanding where the boundaries stand. Where does our responsibility for others lie?

In the movie *Spider-Man 2,* Peter Parker, Spider-Man's alter ego, finds himself stressed and unhappy. His role as Spider-Man, rescuing the city's citizens from crime and disaster, keeps him from sleeping, from developing a relationship with the woman he loves, even from arriving on time to see her perform in a play. The needs around him seem overwhelming, and he begins to burn out. He decides to hang up his Spider-Man suit. But as crime in the city increases 75 percent, Peter is drawn back into his superhero role.

One of the first survival tips for leaders is to recognize our vulnerability to the superhero myth: "If I don't rescue this individual . . . this situation . . . this project, everything will fall apart!" We can go on for months and years carrying other people, until suddenly we can't do it any longer. This way of functioning is the real source of burnout, not overwork. Even Spider-Man finds his web-making powers slipping as he becomes more and more exhausted and overburdened. We can find the powers we do have atrophying, our creativity stifled, as we slog through the routine of burden-bearing leadership.

Whether we are the head of a church, leading a team, or parenting our children, we can get caught up in the needs of others, and lose sight of our own vision and direction. We lurch from crisis to crisis, always reacting, never having the space or time to act with clarity for our most important goals. And, of course, most of us do not have superpowers: we are ordinary human beings. We have gifts of leadership, but we are not that different from those we lead. When we function out of our humanity, recognizing both our strengths and limitations, we make room for others to use their abilities.

Superhero leadership, the charismatic model, does not benefit our organizations or those we lead in the long run. When Spider-Man retires, moves on, or even takes a vacation, what happens? People find themselves unable to function. They have grown complacent and dependent. Their own creativity has been overshadowed by Spider-Man's huge gifts.

What is responsible leadership and what is overresponsible leadership? The clergy leader occupies a unique position; the burdens of pastoral leadership are unavoidable. At the same time, if we are carrying the whole church on our shoulders, we will wear out, and risk crippling our followers. One pastor turned down raises every year during a building program because he thought it would help the church. Not only did the financial sacrifice affect him and his family, it also had a negative effect on the giving level of the congregation for years. Sometimes helping does not really help.

❧ MAINTAINING BALANCE

Family systems theory includes the idea of homeostasis, or balance. Natural systems maintain themselves. If you stretch a rubber band, when you let go, it returns to its original size. When brush starts choking the forest floor, a wildfire sweeps through and cleans it out. Human systems, too, both families and larger groups, achieve a certain balance over time. There is an interdependency among the parts. When one part makes a change, even a positive change, it upsets the balance. The other parts will try to restore the balance. If a leader charts a substantive course forward, parts of the system automatically push back, attempting to restore the balance. To make real progress, one must stay on course in the face of reactions that amount to unintentional sabotage.

For example, a woman who had been home with her children for ten years decided she was ready to go back to work. The first month she was working, one of her children began to show behavior problems at school. Her growth task was not to adapt to the symptom, which might mean quitting her job, but calmly to continue on her own path. She decided to spend more time with her children after work without getting too anxious about the behavior problems, and soon the child settled down at school.

Churches also have their own balance. You never really get away with leadership: when you begin to initiate change, it upsets the balance, which results in a scramble to regain the balance. People are not deliberate or even conscious in this process; they are responding to the upset in the entire system. For example, one pastor found that when he began to state more clearly where he wanted to take the church, people began to criticize his preaching. He was shocked by the response, at first. Then he began to realize the criticism was not about him or his preaching technique. Rather, his new ministry direction has shifted the comfortable balance in the congregation, and people were reacting.

When leaders take a stand, people react automatically. But over time chances are most will come along if the leader calmly stays on course while nurturing relationships with the congregation. This does not mean leaders always get what they want. But it does mean when people react to our positions we should not overreact in response. We stand up and chart a direction, and then we are surprised when people do not automatically cheer and get in line. We have to expect the reaction, not get thrown by it, and stay on track with our goals. The principle of balance tells us that any system will work to restore the status quo. But a consistent, calm effort even in the face of reactivity can begin to make a difference for a congregation.

I have always felt my goal was to promote growth. And if I grow, as I grow, there is a corresponding jump up in the level of maturity of any group I lead. Over time, the point of balance shifts, inch by inch, in the direction of growth. This does not occur without a reaction, even attempted sabotage. And even the best of leaders cannot completely transform a church. But I can make a considerable difference, over time, in helping people function better, with greater maturity.

How does our leadership promote maturity in others? How does the way we chart a course help others grow up? When we are motivated to do good and help others, how do we do it without being invasive? Who is really responsible for the direction of the church?

☙ OVERFUNCTIONING

Family systems thinking also introduces the idea of the over-functioning / underfunctioning reciprocity. An overfunctioner takes too much responsibility, while an underfunctioner does not take enough responsibility. The overfunctioner feels that it is his or her role to see that the underfunctioner shapes up, and the underfunctioner is often perfectly comfortable being dependent. For example, in Christian education a few volunteers often do the lion's share of the work, while leaders try to figure out ways to get those who happily drop off their children to do more.

Overfunctioners and underfunctioners both do their part to maintain this reciprocal balance. Surprisingly, both types are less mature than they should be. Both are unable to determine what is most important for them and follow a clear direction forward. The relationship between the two becomes a dance, where the overfunctioner tries to get the underfunctioner to do more, and the underfunctioner continues to do less.

Overfunctioners are common among clergy and lay leaders. They look at underfunctioners and think, "If they would just shape up, everything would be fine around here." They ask, "Why don't more people volunteer for Sunday school / kitchen duty / visitation / small group leadership?" Then they jump in to fill the gap. A priest proofreads the newsletter every month because the church administrative assistant makes so many mistakes. The women's society president resentfully cleans up the kitchen after every event, because no one else does it well enough.

Reflecting on the concept of overfunctioning, and on my own experience as an overfunctioner, I have concluded that much of what we call "good ministry" is actually overfunctioning. There is a fine line between clear leadership and overfunctioning. When we rush in to help someone, we are not regulating ourselves. Our own anxiety causes us to want to do something, anything—not because we really have a sense of what is best, but because we lack the maturity to sit back and wait. Anxious helping often does not help at all. It does not lead to growth, but to dependency.

The Reverend Cynthia Maybeck, pastor of Trinity Church in Northboro, Massachusetts, says, "To the extent that

I overfunction, it does not give room for people to function. The bottom line of overfunctioning is taking responsibility for other people." She points out that stepping back from overfunctioning is not just about delegating more, or working as a team. There is a deeper level: letting go of responsibility for other people, and even for the success of the institution.

This does not mean we should stop doing good things for people; not all helping is overfunctioning. Everyone needs help at times in life. Here are several characteristics of overfunctioning and underfunctioning to pay attention to:

- When we can only give help and never receive it, we may be overfunctioning.

- If our helpful response comes more from anxiety than from a thoughtful consideration of the best response, we are probably overfunctioning.

- If individuals chronically need help and show no signs of taking responsibility, they are probably underfunctioning.

Offering a challenge may be better than actions we usually consider to be helpful. Expecting more of people at the outset may be more helpful in the long run than doing good things for them. If we get out of their way, they may come up with more creative solutions to their problems than we ever dreamed of, and they will be much better off for having created their own goals. Paul's image of the body of Christ may help here.

> There are many members, yet one body. The eye cannot say to the hand, "I have no need of you," nor again the head to the feet, "I have no need of you." On the contrary, the members of the body that seem to be weaker are indispensable. (1 Corinthians 12:20–22)

The body of Christ provides an image of individuals who are connected together, each responsible for his or her own functioning, and ultimately to Christ as the Head.

If I suggest that I know what is best for others, I usurp their function and limit their functioning. It also keeps me from focusing on myself and on my own functioning. If I spend all my time doing good things for others, I do not have to pay attention to myself. And I may get a lot of attention from others for my good works, too!

Overfunctioning pastoral leaders who get results (especially numerical growth in a congregation) get kudos from denominational leaders. But leaders who take over for others not only risk burning themselves out, they also often limit the growth of others. The subtle challenge is to discern when to chart a bold course, and when to step back so that others can come up with the good ideas. There are no easy answers, but asking the questions rather than immediately assuming we know best is a good start.

Leaders make a difference by the nature of their presence in the system, not by anxiously trying to fix everything and everyone. This is true whether they are relating to their family, the congregation, the denomination, or society at large. They live out of themselves rather than living through others. This focus on self is not selfish, because our self, who we are, is God-given. And the more I become myself, my truly mature self, the more I will be able to call others to maturity. In order to follow the commandment to "love your neighbor as yourself" (Mark 12:31), we must *be* a self.

❧ SPIRITUAL TEACHINGS FOR LEADERS

The idea of managing the responsibility of spiritual leaders is not new. Two ancient writers, as interpreted in the modern era, may offer us guidance in this matter. According to Joan Chittister, the Rule of St. Benedict suggests an approach for leaders that makes room for challenge as well as support, and does not foster dependency. Chittister points out:

Benedict wants a community that is led, but not driven. The concept is clear: people are not acquitted of the responsibility for their own souls. Personal decisions are still decisions, personal judgments are still judgments, free will is still free will. Being in a family does not relieve a child of the responsibility to grow up. The function of twenty-one-year-olds is not to do life's tasks as their parents told them to when they were six years old. The function of twenty-one-year-olds is simply to do the same tasks well and to take accountability themselves for having done them. . . . The role of leadership is not to make lackeys or foot soldiers or broken children out of adult Christians.[2]

Each of us must ultimately find our own way. It is irresponsible and arrogant to presume to know that way for another. And to put it positively, we can be the most help by giving people space to find creative solutions to their own struggles. As Garret Keizer puts it in *Help: The Original Human Dilemma,* sometimes the answer to the question "What would Jesus do?" is "Nothing."

Psychiatrist Gerald May discusses the ideas of St. John of the Cross in an article titled "Don't Be a Pest." Four hundred years ago, John offered advice to the spiritual directors of people who were moving toward deeper awareness of God, and were in distress as a result. John says directors often know only how to "hammer and pound" with practices and concepts that "they themselves have used or read of somewhere." These "pestiferous" directors work against the exquisite gift God is giving. May uses this example from John of the Cross:

Images and perceptions of God disappear. A person might say, "God used to be very real for me as a loving Presence, but now all I find is emptiness and void." Spiritual directors may desperately want to help fill this void for others, but John says it would be a mistake to try to do so. . . . Putting it succinctly, he says, "God does not fit in an occupied heart."[3]

It shows us that real spiritual implications exist in our over-functioning, our getting in the space of others.

What could be more ethically questionable than interfering in another's relationship with God? Yet I must plead guilty as I think of the times I have been made so anxious by a person's spiritual crisis that I would have done anything to make it better. I remember one day dropping all my plans on my day off to rush to the home of a church member when she called me in crisis. "I'm so glad you're here," she said in relief. But as we talked longer, I realized my quick response was not that helpful. She had more resources than I realized, but now she was depending on me.

For those of us with a lifetime of practice in pestering others and doing things for their own good, this new approach is not easy. We may feel we are being cold, unfeeling, unchristian, even unethical! We assume that not helping means we are bad people; we are programmed to help. Those of us who enter professional ministry are probably as thoroughly programmed as anyone. Can we learn to trust God with the lives of others?

❧ FAMILY PATTERNS

I learned my own tendency to overfunction early. As the oldest daughter of an oldest daughter who was a preacher's daughter, my position in my family prepared me to take responsibility for others. When my anxiety goes up, my overfunctioning and my irritability with the perceived underfunctioning ("irresponsibility!") of others increase. In commenting on this common tendency, pastoral counselor James Boyer says, "I think several things can be helpful to the clergy who find themselves being overhelpful with others. It can be useful for clergy to identify who in their family they were trained to rescue so as not to mistake legitimate professional helping with illegitimate family rescuing—which is inevitably tied to unhealthy ways of trying to feel good about oneself."

When we grimly take responsibility for everything and everyone, we invite burnout. Being a good leader and being extremely serious are not identical, and can even be mutually exclusive. A light touch goes a long way toward clarifying what we need to do for others and helping others hear what we say as leader. This relaxed attitude comes from personal security, which can come from faith. If we live out of trust in God, we can relax—we do not have to worry about taking care of everyone, because the results do not depend on us.

I found I had plenty of opportunities to practice this the year my daughter prepared to go to college. I had to restrain myself (not always successfully) from rushing in to offer suggestions or to remind her of deadlines, but I also knew her success in life, in college, or even in the application process did not depend on me. Fortunately, she was quite good at setting the boundaries. In one conversation, when I was fussing at her about the upcoming financial aid form deadlines, I finally got enough distance to ask her, "What would really help you?" She answered, "Just do for me what I can't do for myself, and let me do the rest. I can worry about deadlines plenty on my own." She was clear and self-defined. No doubt I learned more in this process than she did. Perhaps we can say to others, "I will only do for you what you cannot do for yourself."

The tricky part of this is we get a lot of credit for taking responsibility for others. And when we decide to step back from that role, people seldom thank us; in fact, they may do just the opposite. Cynthia Maybeck says, "When we stop overfunctioning, it rocks the institution, because the expectation is that we will." Many churches are organized around the overresponsibility of clergy and other key lay leaders, who then risk burnout, only to be replaced by others who fill the same role. James Boyer also suggests, "It's probably a good idea for clergy who like helping to increase their tolerance of others' disappointment in them. Another way to say this is for clergy to practice receiving the disappointment of others as neutrally as possible—that is less personally. I find that clergy who are at least as passionate about their own needs as they are about the needs of others seem to do much better overall."

≈ HELPING THAT HELPS

In reflecting on the help I have received that has truly helped, I find that the people who have been the most useful show particular qualities:

1) They stay calm.

2) They ask more questions and give less advice.

3) They do not have too much invested in how I do. They are happy when I start doing better, but their sense of self is not dependent on my actions.

When I am the helper and can stay in that same place myself, I find I am more good to others, too. Here are five tips for relating to people at times of need:

1) Challenge people to grow through their difficulties.
Don't stop at handholding, but help them to develop emotionally and spiritually.

2) Watch for the neediest people.
While they need support, they can use up a huge proportion of ministry resources (including your energy) and still come back needing more and more and more. Practice saying "no" to repeat customers.

3) Find those who are resourceful in the face of personal challenge.
Look for ways to develop their gifts and help them find ministries of their own.

4) Know your own family history.
We bring our own family emotional baggage, too. When we are aware of our own emotional "hooks," we are more able to be present and genuinely helpful to people rather than mindlessly rescuing them.

5) Hone your awareness of time spent with people.
This will vary with your job description, the size of the church, and the nature of the pastoral need. But our own anxiety can cause us either to want to bolt too quickly or to spend hours with people when they may not need it.

In the gospels, Jesus always gives people space, and makes space for himself. Jesus, more than anyone else, was able to live out of a position of relaxed trust. He simply said, "Your sins are forgiven. Go and sin no more." If Jesus himself can give room to others, without chasing after them for their own good, perhaps we, too, can begin to do the same.

Paul tells the Christians in Philippi to "work out your own salvation with fear and trembling" (Philippians 2:12). As their leader, he urges the church at Philippi to obey him, but he also acknowledges that the responsibility for their lives is ultimately their own. Yet elsewhere he writes, "Bear one another's burdens and in this way you will fulfill the law of Christ" (Galatians 6:2). How can we obey both these injunctions? As we mature, emotionally and in the faith, we are better able to deal with tension and ambiguity. Should we bear another's burdens or challenge them to work out their salvation? It depends! As Gerald May put it, don't be a pest!

✎ QUESTIONS TO PONDER
Understanding our responsibility both in leadership and pastoral care (which are related) means knowing we are ultimately responsible for ourselves before God. We have the care of a congregation and of the individuals within it in our charge, yet if we carry them ourselves we will stumble and

fall, to no one's advantage. The world may need superheroes, but I am not one and probably you are not either. Chances are you do not need an alter ego superhero. You only need to be yourself. Being yourself is sustainable. Being a superhero is not.

Here are five questions for you to consider about over-functioning:

- In what relationships am I taking too much responsibility?

- How might I step back, at least a little?

- Did I learn to overfunction in my family? How do I understand that part of my story?

- In any given situation, how can I learn to ask, "What might help this person grow?"

- If I were to take less responsibility for others, what would I do with my time and energy?

CHAPTER 3

KNOW YOUR
CHURCH'S STORY

On a trip to Kansas for a family reunion, my parents, my brother, and I made our way to the farm property that used to be in my grandmother's family. My great-great-grandparents had settled the land in the 1870s, moving from Ohio to central Kansas to homestead. We drove down the dusty gravel road, between the tawny stalks of wheat, along a route that had been used for generations, first for horse-drawn wagons, then pickups and tractors, and finally our silver rental car.

Congregations also have well-worn pathways, sometimes set down by early settlers, sometimes developed along the way. These paths can be healthy and beneficial, like support and encouragement for pastors, open communication in times of crisis, or the ability to incorporate newcomers easily. Other patterns are not so useful, such as secrecy around difficult issues, persistent conflict between clergy and lay leaders, or key members leaving when things get tough. We need to be well aware of the past pathways in our particular setting as we travel the path to the future.

❧ THE PRESENCE OF THE PAST

It is important to remember "the presence of the past," as scientist Rupert Sheldrake calls it. Patterns are established over time, and old problems (and old solutions) of a congregation are likely to crop up again. The past need not determine the future, but if we ignore it, we are more likely to be tripped up by it, as powerful patterns persist without our awareness. Better to be curious, to look for the threads that continue and experiment with ways we might claim and use them without being governed by them.

When we do not know the past, we can find ourselves frustrated by dynamics that do not make sense to us. As a pastor, I found myself struggling, like so many others, to help my small church grow in numbers. One day when I was reviewing some old records, however, I discovered a pastor's letter that showed attendance on a World Communion Sunday in the 1930s had been exactly the same as it was on World Communion Sunday that year! I was stunned to see the parallel. Furthermore, I learned that for years the church had hovered around the same attendance.

Edwin Friedman used the phrase "the persistence of form" to talk about how hard it is to change patterns that are set—whether it is the struggle to lose weight, to affect the size of a congregation, or to modify the ways people relate to one another in families or institutions. The persistence of form was at work in my church, too. This was not just about the success or failure of my efforts or of any particular church growth program. Nor was it simply the recalcitrance of church people who "just didn't want to grow." Something larger was going on. Systems find ways to maintain their shape and size.

Another church I know well has a history of strong lay leadership, with periodic conflict between lay leaders and pastors. This pattern has lasted for generations. Knowing that cycle can help both clergy and lay leaders keep perspective on the shifting relationships within the church. And it can help pastors avoid taking the conflict personally by understanding that something deeper is at work in the congregation.

We might wonder why parishioners will not go along with this or that program, because to us it is the only direction that makes sense. Then we discover that the three previous pastors tried to shove denominational initiatives down the congregation's throat. We need to realize there's something bigger than us going on here!

Or we might focus our attention on people who seem to be the problem, labeling them as difficult, or even antagonistic. We think that if we could just get rid of them, then everything would be different. But it always takes two to tango: the problem is not simply with a difficult person, but with the relationship we have with them. Our response contributes to the difficulties. And the difficult relationship may be "in the water," part of the historic patterns of that congregation.

What happens *between* people matters at least as much as what happens *inside* people, and this is true down the generations. In church life, relationships cross generations, just as in families. A church is not a family, despite our frequent references to the "church family," yet many of the same relationship processes are at work. And, of course, more than almost any other institution, many congregations have multigenerational families within them so the dynamics can become more intense than in other organizations. In one church, the congregation president took a stand in a conflict that led to his mother-in-law leaving the church and blaming him. For leaders to keep their heads amid this kind of intensity takes both clear thinking and a strong stomach.

So, as Friedman pointed out, an individual can leave a congregation and someone else can begin to act the same way, even if he or she did not know the one who left. One pastor was relieved when her nemesis left the congregation and moved away. Her relief lasted only until she began to wonder, "Who's going to come and take his place?" And in fact, someone was already ready to take over as prime antagonist. She felt that paying attention to these dynamics as well as her own emotional growth helped her. She found herself less intimidated and more relaxed about the situation the second time around. But the pattern persisted in the congregation: her successor also got caught in a battle with two key leaders.

In the congregation where I am a recent member, I became the chair of a structure task force. As we concluded our work, I discovered to my surprise that there had been two structure task forces in recent years, neither of which had had any impact. Ultimately, neither did our task force. I also learned in the process that Major Robert, author of *Robert's Rules of Order,* had been an influential member of the congregation in the nineteenth century, organizing the Sunday school. The bureaucratic nature of this congregation is deeply entrenched, and will not be easily shifted.

Larger institutions also show the same multigenerational dynamics at work. When the Episcopal Diocese of Newark was searching for a new bishop, the committee did some research on previous bishops. The diocese has been known for its liberal and often controversial bishop who retired in 2000, John Spong. To their surprise, they discovered a long history of liberal bishops committed to social concerns and varied viewpoints, including one in the early twentieth century who was known for his "beautiful tolerance for the beliefs of others." The commitment to social concern dated back to the time of the Revolutionary War, when the diocese needed to deal with the postwar fallout after many battles were fought in New Jersey. The diocese's focus on theological openness and social justice ministry has its roots deep in the past.[4]

THE FOUNDING STORY

The founding of a church lays down patterns that show up in the present. If a church begins by splitting off from another congregation, the memory of that split becomes embedded in that congregation. In churches and denominations that fled persecution in another country, some survival anxiety persists through the generations into the future. A church that is founded with heavy financial support from the denomination without enough challenge to stewardship can develop a passive attitude toward giving that lasts for years.

One downtown church took over fifteen years to become self-supporting. The first pastor did not work out, and worship ceased twice during those fifteen years. For a time one key family made up the only members of the church. Once the church got off the ground, however, it had a large and significant ministry for decades. Then in the 1970s, as with many downtown churches, things began to decline, and there were struggles with the pastors. Finally the church called a strong pastor who stayed for over twenty years. A significant conflict broke out under the next pastor, who stayed less than two years.

Conventional thinking would see this as a typical response to a successor of a long-term pastor. I would go further, however, and suggest that at the beginning, some survival anxiety was programmed into the congregation when they had such a bumpy start. When attendance began to decline in the 1970s, that survival anxiety reemerged, leading to a difficult relationship with a couple of pastors. The next pastor, a very strong leader, held it together. When he left the anxiety rose again, making it hard for people to make thoughtful decisions. The result was a call to an excellent pastor who was not a good fit. The challenges faced by the church were not merely about the momentary crisis of losing a long-term pastor, but were rooted in the history of the church from the beginning.

Churches, like families, tend to exhibit certain symptoms. In some families, for example, alcoholism is the perennial symptom: we all know families where alcoholism persists throughout generations. In churches, there may be a history of conflict over a particular issue, like music or worship, or over people in particular positions, like the minister. Some churches have more serious symptoms, such as a history of ministers who violate sexual boundaries. Some churches have a pattern of firing their ministers—or of treating them very well. Recognizing the patterns can give a sense of perspective about the challenges we are facing. We can see that it is not all about us. And we can develop appropriate humility about what we can and cannot change. Leadership is critically important, but leaders are not all-powerful in the face of deep patterns with a long history.

❧ FINDING THE STRENGTHS

On that Kansas farm my family saw something else—oil wells pumping. Yes, we shared a moment of regret that the property was no longer in the family. But I have to admire whoever realized wheat was not the only potential resource. Someone dug deep, went beyond the usual, and now, decades later, oil is still coming out of the ground.

My Kansas family faced many challenges generations ago, and ultimately lost the property (not to mention the oil buried deep beneath). The paths of anxiety laid down then still run deep in the family. But other resources as well—the pioneer spirit, the ability to relocate easily, and the connection with family across distance—are also deeply embedded in us.

Churches have persistent patterns of anxiety, as we have seen, but they also have resources deep within: the sense of purpose the founders had, a faith tradition that has sustained them for decades, a respect for leadership. A church that loses its building to fire experiences a traumatic event, but may also find the resilience to rebuild. That sense of resourcefulness will continue to be present in the congregation as they build new ministries for the future. Humans are enormously creative and resilient. The resources lurk beneath the surface, just like the oil beneath my family's field.

One church I worked with, St. Mark's Episcopal Church in Teaneck, New Jersey, found that cooperation with the Roman Catholic hospital next door always seemed to work like a charm. Everything they did together was successful. The rector, the Reverend Randall Day, learned that the same woman who gave the land for the church in the 1920s also gave the land for the hospital. He says, "As she saw it, these places would serve the community. Their purpose found their original meaning in Grace Chadwick's visionary intention." The two institutions share a historic connection that makes new things possible in the present.

Over time, we may find that the old boundary lines are still used, but in some new ways. Wheat and oil can come from the same land, both providing energy for human consumption. The old and the new can exist side by side. It is important to find the stories of achievement and possibility, and to tell them to those in the present as a way to access the forces for resilience and renewal that are still present. The old stories can lay the groundwork for new ministry in the future.

Augustana Lutheran Church, in Portland, Oregon, is a vital urban congregation with a strong focus on multicultural ministry and social justice. The church recently opened a time capsule that the congregation closed up in 1907. It included the statement, "The women have a right to vote in the congregation." Also included was the September 14, 1907, issue of *The Oregonian,* the Portland daily newspaper, with an article about the challenges faced by Hindu immigrants from India. Pastor Mark Knutson says, "Finding the two pieces was good for our congregation as we try to step out in new ways of justice. To hear them say one hundred years ago, fourteen years before women's suffrage, this is a congregation where women have the right to vote, was very powerful and offered strength for today. The same with the article about the persecution of Hindu immigrants: to hear Swedish immigrants lifting up an article like this, again a statement from one hundred years ago, speaks to the need today for true immigration reform." Augustana's current ministries are in continuity with the past in ways they did not even realize.

◈ LEADING WITH THE PAST IN MIND

Understanding the congregation's history plays an important role in staying calm and flexible as a leader. Make this a project: to know the history and the patterns and acknowledge their presence, while still keeping somewhat free of them. This will give you the strength and the credibility to step outside of them thoughtfully when needed.

Murray Bowen, one of the founders of the family therapy movement, highlighted the predictable patterns in families and other human groups when someone begins to act in new, growth-producing ways. People react—"You're stepping off the path, get back on it"—before they are able to follow. They may even try to pull the leader back on the path, instinctively creating a crisis, for example, in order to suck him or her back into the old ways of doing things. But if the leader can work on these relationships while still affirming the value of trying new paths, there is a good chance people will come along, though they will no doubt be glancing over their shoulders at the old, lovely, and familiar ways even as they follow. Change is evolutionary, not revolutionary. As a pastor, I developed a mantra: "Everything takes five years." Substantial developments in congregational life, the kind that will last, take even longer.

I have found that understanding the power of the past is both humbling and freeing. I begin to see that I do not have as much power as I think to make things happen the way I would like. And I begin to see I am part of an organic process of being the church through the generations, and this particular church over the years. I make my small contribution. Others have gone before me and will come after me. I am part of the stream of the life of the church, and of this church, so I am freer to let go and allow the flow to happen. I still need to work hard for my own vision, and pay attention to my relationships. But at the same time, the pressure to produce is less intense when I can take the long view, both looking back and looking forward.

Position yourself as a researcher in the congregation, an archaeologist who is unearthing the layers. You will gain more neutrality about the intense issues in the present and the past, which will help you think more clearly about possibilities and pitfalls for the future. Your role in this process is to tease out the history, initially for yourself. You will be a calmer leader if you have access to this broader perspective. Over time you can be thoughtful about how to share the perspective you gain. Telling stories about the past, especially the strengths and successes, can be a source of vitality for a congregation. Telling secrets, of course, can be fraught with danger. Greater openness is generally better than less, but trying to force people to face the truth rarely helps.

Every congregation is fascinating. When we can remain curious about our church's story, past and present, we will be less likely to become willful or frustrated, distant or burned out. Ask yourself, "How can I tease out what it is they do, and when? What are the patterns that I see?"

❧ QUESTIONS TO PONDER

The author of the letter to the Hebrews wrote, "Therefore, since we are surrounded by so great a cloud of witnesses, let us also lay aside every weight and the sin that clings so closely, and let us run with perseverance the race that is set before us" (12:1). Taking the witness of the past seriously is a way of seeing the future both realistically and hopefully. As we will see next, our own family story affects our ministry profoundly. The past does not determine the future, but it has an influence. We do not stop with the past, of course, or even the present. The past is a prelude to the future. Clear thinking in the present and vision for the future are critically important to lasting leadership.

Here are ten questions to consider as you look at your church's story:

- Who carries the memory and how might I connect with them? (It can be worth mapping out on paper.)

- What was my church's focus at the founding? What stories have been passed down from that time?

- What strands do I see in the present that stretch back to the past?

- Who were the leaders, clergy and lay, official and unofficial, and what was their tenure? What were the circumstances of the departures of key leaders?

- What significant events have marked the way—big successes or major traumas?

- What is the relationship of the congregation with the wider denominational family?

- What are the issues that become the focus of anxiety (worship, music, youth)?

- What is the history of the congregation with relation to its building or buildings?

- How open is the church with regard to sharing information (about financial matters, for example)? What secrets might there be? Who knows the secrets?

- How can I use the stories of the past to strengthen the congregation, and myself, in the present?

CHAPTER 4

KNOW YOUR OWN STORY

A minister leaves church on Sunday, fuming. The congregation president has just resigned suddenly, and the minister feels let down. Somehow this always seems to happen to him, especially with men who are older leaders in the church. "Why can't these guys be more committed?" he complains to his wife. What he does not realize is how these men in the church trigger his childhood longing to be closer to his distant father; consequently he has this experience in church after church. Many church leaders get beaten up or burned out, and even leave ministry disillusioned, because they do not understand how church systems work, and do not understand themselves well enough.

Most of us have walked away from an encounter with a church member thinking, "What just happened there?" To make our relationships in ministry less of a pitfall and more of a delight, we have to know ourselves. What do you notice about yourself as you relate to people in ministry? When you can recognize your responses and connect what you do with patterns in your family of origin, you can gain valuable insight and gradually improve your leadership.

❧ OUR FAMILY STORY

Relationships are both the most delightful and the hardest part of ministry. We all learn how to relate to others in the family we grow up in. For better and for worse, this is what feels normal and natural. We learn how to respond to others, and we get emotional buttons programmed into us. Dr. Lawrence Matthews, who works with clergy to apply family systems thinking to ministry and leadership, suggests that at birth you walk on the stage, and the play's well underway. They hand you the script, and you go along with the script. When we get into parish life and the same script is enacted, we react automatically without even realizing we are hooked. When we unconsciously act from our family script, our choices are limited. It tells us how to be angry, or how to hide, or how to protect others. We learned our lines as soon as we learned to talk.

To be most effective, both as a leader and in pastoral care, church leaders need to understand their own family history and the impact it has on what they do in the present. What are your hooks, your emotional vulnerabilities? Understanding your family and learning to be more neutral about it is a long process. This learning will help your leadership in your congregation more than anything else you can do. It will help you help the families under your care. When you are less reactive to your family, you will also be less reactive at church. You will be calmer and clearer, both of which make for better leadership.

Many clergy are oldest children. They learn early to over-function in relation to others, to take responsibility for them. Jan is an oldest daughter, with a father and brother who underfunctioned in the family. She discovered the degree to which her male associate was not measuring up only when other leaders in the church pointed it out to her. She was so used to males underperforming that she could not even see it.

Frank is a highly responsible oldest son who found himself in a frustrating relationship with a senior minister who never seemed to provide a clear vision. Frank's father also underfunctioned and had trouble providing for the family. Frank's relationship with his boss replicated his experience at home.

Tom, on the other hand, is the youngest member of his family, with several older brothers and sisters who treated him almost as a puppy or favorite toy while he was growing up. As a result he finds it difficult to be a clear and defined leader, and tends to wait for other leaders in the church to make the first move. The members of his congregation are just as frustrated with him as he is with them, and the church's ministry languishes.

Birth order is only one of the dynamics that affect us. There are many issues that move down the generations within families, such as physical illness, conflict between spouses, and cutting off important relationships. A priest who grew up in a family with a lot of physical illness may take too much responsibility in helping others who are sick. If conflict between spouses is a frequent family pattern, a pastoral leader may find herself mediating the conflicts of others in the church. If the family response is distance or cutoff, another minister may find it hard to stay emotionally connected to his congregation. He may end up with a series of short pastorates because he encouraged distance in the relationship or looked for a new church when things got difficult.

We often do not realize we are following these patterns because they are so automatic. They feel normal, and we are most comfortable when we are in these roles, even when we complain about them. "I'm the only one who takes responsibility around here." "Why can't they just get along?" "I'm ready to get my deployment papers ready again—I've had enough." Yet the patterns limit our leadership. When my goal as a pastoral leader was to avoid conflict at all costs, I could not provide my congregation with the kind of vision and direction they needed. The script we learned in childhood is deeply ingrained, and it will never completely go away. Yet we can learn, little by little, to have a wider repertoire, to respond less automatically.

Of course, not all the things we learn from our families are negative. Some of the old patterns are tremendous gifts. Edwin Friedman used to ask, "What gifts did your parents give to you?" Growth can come when we seek to build on the strengths of the past. For example, Bishop Thomas Shaw of the Episcopal Diocese of Massachusetts says of his family, "My father had a tremendous sense of loyalty and faithfulness. My parents had a long, rich marriage. I think that kind of dogged loyalty has really helped me understand that you stay with things, and you don't back out. With both of them the idea was you make a commitment and then you see it through."

My own mother is extremely hospitable at church. Greeting people and welcoming them is second nature to her—and also to me. Both my parents are very open to people and curious about them. Every time they come to visit they tell me about the fascinating people they talked with at the airport and on the plane. Asking people questions about themselves and drawing them out is also very easy for me. I find these are great assets in my ministry.

What does it mean to explore our family story? Why should we bother? It is hard emotional work. Our internal resistance to this work can be great. It may cost money and vacation time to travel to visit family we have not seen for a long time. As pastoral counselor Ron Richardson notes:

> Most of us hesitate to do this. We fear getting trapped or swallowed up in that family system. The more resistant people are to doing family work, the more likely they are to be emotionally trapped in that system, even while keeping their distance. The fact is that we don't grow up and become mature by staying away from those people. We gain emotional separation and maturity by getting closer to them and working at being a self in their presence.[5]

♒ LEARNING ABOUT OUR FAMILY

The more we learn about our family story, the more we learn about ourselves. We begin to get a fuller picture of our family through the generations, the patterns we may never have noticed, and the choices our parents and grandparents made that affect us to this day. In Genesis God calls Abraham to "the land I will show you," and Abraham's decision to follow affects the lives of generations to come. In a way, exploring our family story is like entering a new land. Familiar territory becomes unfamiliar as we look at the same old story with new eyes. This takes courage akin to Abraham's.

The initial step in looking at our family story is to create a family diagram or genogram.[6] Looking at a minimum of three generations, and ideally more, will help you begin to understand some of the processes that took place over time in your family. Some of these facts we learn growing up, while other stories are never talked about or have long been forgotten. Beginning to ask these questions of family members puts us in a new position in our family already. All this takes time: assessing the multigenerational processes is not a one-time project, but a long-term effort.

When I looked at my initial family diagram, I realized my family was very comfortable with geographic moves. I moved from the west coast to the east to serve a church as pastor. As a woman, this was the only way I could find a church to lead in my denomination. I noticed that people in my family have moved all over the place, on both sides of my family. I realized it was no wonder I could move to a church across the country without a lot of apparent emotional upheaval.

Over the years as I have assessed my family in greater depth, I have realized that geographical moves sometimes serve as a way for people to distance emotionally. I have also seen that while I made a big move easily, there was a price to be paid for being so distant from my own family of origin. My husband and I both struggled with depression over the

37

years, intensified as a consequence of being disconnected from our families.

As I continued to explore, I noticed how distant we had been from my father's family my entire life. The last time we visited my father's parents, I was ten. They died within about six months of each other in my mid-teens, and my father traveled alone to the funeral. At the time, I saw nothing unusual in that. As I learned about the multigenerational history of my father's family, however, I found out more about a tragic event in previous generations, when my paternal great-grandfather killed himself and his wife. My father did not learn about this event until he was grown, and he did not tell my brother and me about it until we were grown.

As these aspects of family life move into our conscious awareness, we experience a shift in perspective. Problems do not magically disappear, yet we can begin a slow evolution. We can have more choices in how we relate to people. When we can be more thoughtful and less reactive in our relationships, the outcome will be better. Psychotherapist Elaine Boomer says of this work, "The hopeful part is awareness, because if you are aware, you can change. If you have no awareness there's no possibility of change."

For example, I found as I explored the difficult history of my family, I was less afraid of conflict at church or of people being angry with me. I made decisions more in the best interests of the ministry and less as a way of avoiding conflict. I initiated difficult conversations sooner, rather than postponing them in the vain hope that the problem would go away. I took stands with staff instead of letting them do whatever they wanted to. I became a stronger leader.

In this process, I began to think about connecting with my father's side of the family, in order to continue to understand myself and the family story. I made my first visit to my grandparents' grave. On my return home, I found myself asking for, negotiating, and being granted a sabbatical leave for the following summer, something completely new for my congregation. This made me wonder, moreover, whether my sense of clarity and calm through that process was related to those moments of connection with my grandparents, even though they were no longer living. I had missed their funeral, but I had finally paid my respects. Even when pledged giving to the church for the year of my sabbatical dropped, for the first time in my ten-year ministry there, I felt calm instead of panicky. My calmer response helped others stay calm, and giving rebounded quickly.

I knew the most important task of that sabbatical was to visit my uncle, my father's brother, whom I had not seen since I was ten. Sabbatical seminars, travel to Costa Rica, and professional books were also in the plan, yet those activities had far less relevance. I first visited his daughter, my first cousin, who lived near a conference I was attending on sabbatical. Then I visited my uncle, who was delighted to see me. When I returned from sabbatical, therefore, I was refreshed and rested. More importantly, I felt well able to deal with the post-sabbatical bumpiness at the church. When the deacons started squabbling during my first meeting back, it did not throw me. I felt less anxious in general and clearer about who I wanted to be as a pastor.

I planned a trip the next summer to Kansas, where my father had been born. We visited his cousins, and stayed with one of them on their farmhouse surrounded by cornfields. Cousin Bill showed us all the boyhood haunts that still exist, and one day we drove out to Lyons, where my father had been born. My great-grandparents are buried there; their murder-suicide took place in this town. I went into the town clerk's office to find the cemetery records. Looking at the book, the young woman at the desk asked in surprise, "They died on the same day—was it an accident?" I answered, "No, it was a murder-suicide," and suddenly a powerful sense of shame enveloped me. I realized, if not in that moment, then soon afterward, that this was my grandmother's shame. She walked around the town with that shame for all the years afterward that she lived there, and probably for the rest of her life.

The legacy of that event, I began to realize, is my fear of conflict, and the desire to avoid having people be mad at me. I knew that about myself and I knew it limited my ministry, but I did not know why it was true. Since that visit, I have been able to face conflict in a new way. Edwin Friedman used to speak about a client, a former boxer, who said boxing was not about being able to take a punch, but about loving a punch. I am not sure I will ever be able to love a punch, but I can take it a lot better than I used to. I know the old patterns are still there and reemerge in times of higher stress. Yet I have more tools to put to work to deal with them, and I can recognize the signs sooner and recover more quickly from missteps.

☙ FAMILY AS A RESOURCE

As you engage in family of origin work over time, you can begin to assess and become more neutral about the dynamics in your family of origin. Along with the difficulties, it is important to consider the gifts. The Reverend Meg Hess, teacher of preaching and leadership and a pastoral counselor, says, "I feel more compassionate toward my family. I'm less in a position of blaming them and more in a position to appreciate what they gave me and their strengths, rather than focusing on their failings. It's a process of moving from resentment to gratitude."

You can even think about how your family might be a resource for you in your ministry, if they are still living. You might imagine what advice your agnostic father might give you about a problem with the board president. Or you might call up your mother to share a staff challenge. She might have useful advice—and simply asking the question can begin to shift the relationship. More flexibility in relationships helps everyone in the family, including ourselves.

I began asking my younger brother, who had taken a long break from church, for occasional advice. As the older sister, I gave him advice until he was at least thirty; old habits die hard! When I started asking him for advice, he seemed surprised and pleased, and he always gave me good ideas. Because of his corporate experience he had a perspective on organizational relationships that I did not always have, and his input was valuable. For example, I asked him about a worrying conflict that had erupted in the church over a youth program; I was anxious that the children in the youth group, particularly my own daughter, would be upset by the conflict. Joe said, "They are probably tougher than you think. Maybe they will learn something from it." Immediately I realized this was good advice, and I calmed down. The conflict simply faded away without any action on my part.

Your family may know nothing about your ministry. If so, telling someone in your family exactly what you do for a living can be a powerful way to connect with them. Whether or not they express interest, saying more of who we really are to our families without expecting anything in return helps us grow up. Or, if you come from a long line of ministers in the same denomination, calmly stating where you differ from the party line is another way to say something of who you are to your family.

Family work is never easy, and even after many years we can still encounter resistance. For a family visit, three days is about right. It is hard to maintain any neutrality for longer than that. Remember, this is not "six weeks to a new family life": this is a long-term project. We can stay at it for our own growth, and also for our grandchildren, great-nieces, and great-nephews, with the conviction that our own work will benefit future generations and gift them with greater freedom. And when we are able to define ourselves clearly in the families we grew up in, we will find greater clarity in our vision as leaders. Larry Matthews describes this as "defining yourself in the place that defined you."

☜ THE CRUCIBLE OF FAMILY LIFE

The crucible of our family life has forged our leadership. Even if we think we left home years ago and never went back, we carry the struggles and strengths with us daily. If we are cut off emotionally from our families, or are overly close to them, we will find it more challenging to develop clarity and perspective as a leader and to relate well to those we lead.

In family systems theory, "fusion" and "cutoff" are identified as two of the ways families deal with anxiety. When family members—mother and daughter, husband and wife— are too close, fusion takes place. It begins with the fusion of infant and mother, and we all still experience it to one degree or another. We recognize the extremes: everyone knows long-married couples who come to look like each other. Couples will speak for each other or begin each sentence with "we." Or extended family members will all live within a block or two of each other.

The flip side of the coin is emotional cutoff. People become so emotionally reactive to each other that they have to distance themselves from one another and may even break off contact. For example, a son moves across the country and rarely calls or writes, coming home once every five years. He may think he is being independent, but in fact he is dealing with the intensity in his relationship with his parents by staying away. A brother and sister who live in the same town do not speak to each other. A family gathers only at holidays, exchanging only superficial greetings.

When our family relationships reflect one of these two extremes, our effectiveness as leaders will be lessened. We will be less able to find clarity and to discern our unique vision and contribution. We will be more reactive to those who criticize us, or accept without question the adulation of those who agree with us. We will be overly dependent on others for our sense of ourselves. Both emotional distance and emotional fusion or over-closeness are ways of managing anxiety in relationship. When we are able to stand in a different place in relation to others, moving a step away or a step closer, we may find ourselves experiencing more anxiety. The old ways of relating are familiar and comfortable, and experimenting with new ways is not easy.

Still, as we have the courage to step into a different place in the families we grew up in, we will find over time a new clarity of direction in our ministry. We will be less likely to wonder anxiously, "Will they or won't they follow?" as we step out in new directions. The clearer we are, the less stress we will experience. As we lead from a deep place of personal centeredness, we will find new energy and vitality, little by little. This process is not an easy one, and it is never over. Progress is often by inches rather than in great strides. Over time we can find, however, that we make significant shifts in the way we function in all our important relationships.

～ FAMILY WORK IS HARD WORK

We cannot increase our own sense of clarity and our maturity as human beings and as leaders without some struggle. We have to increase our tolerance for our own pain and not merely look for the quick fix. The Reverend Keith Harder, a pastor in the Mennonite Church USA, has been exploring his family story for seven or eight years. He says about the process, "It's both helpful and sobering because I realize how deeply ingrained some of these patterns are. But a little bit of change and a little bit of awareness goes a long way. So I don't get too hung up on that."

Then Harder adds, "I think I am more in touch with how anxious my family was, and how I experienced that, especially in my adolescence. There was a lot of conflict between mom and dad, a lot of unpredictability. I never knew when he'd be around, and what mood he'd be in when he was around. I found myself in a mediating role, and confidant and companion of my mother.

"So a classic rescuing, over-responsible, overfunctioning pattern of behavior took root early, and it was exacerbated when my sisters left home—they married young and left by the time I was eight or nine. I've come to see how much that shaped my relationships, and especially my functioning in ministry and leadership roles. I have quickly found myself gravitating to function in overly responsible ways, and more than I like to admit for a long time, a certain conflict avoidance." Harder notes that he is now able to recognize it more quickly and tone down the intensity, so as to get a little better perspective on it. "Family of origin work," he concludes, "has helped my functioning in leadership and other relationships."

Harder finds that the family of origin work never ends. He began systematically to interview some of his first cousins about his father. He recalls, "It was amazing to me how my dad become more three-dimensional, more textured. When I could see how others saw him as generous and fun-loving, and how they really admired him in ways that I never expected, it was really useful to me to have that image expanded.

"It helped some things to break loose. Right before I was going to make a presentation to some pastors, including telling some of my own story, I had a dream I was telling my dad what I was learning, and in that dream he was really interested in what I was learning. I have claimed that as something breaking loose in me, that somehow that fearful child that was always yearning for his affirmation and recognition was beginning to grow up a bit."

So the hard work begins at home, in our family of origin. The good news is that it is never too late to start. Even if you have no surviving family, you can work on reconnecting with memories, even painful ones. You can seek out more distant relatives to connect with. Do you know your cousins? Are your aunts and uncles still living?

We do have to be willing to make people uncomfortable when we enter this process. Sometimes we have to ask about things people would rather not talk about. All human systems have a powerful balance. When the balance changes, forces kick in to try to restore the balance. When we step into a new place in our family, it upsets the balance. And the family will react in predictable ways. It may come through criticism ("How dare you ask that question?") or through seduction ("I love you so much; please bail your brother out one more time"). Throughout the process we will inevitably get emotionally hooked in. At those points we can try cultivating humor, breathing deeply, and reminding ourselves of our goals, which can help us keep on track.

Here are some suggestions for the journey home:

Don't try to fix anyone.
Enter your family as a researcher, curious about what you can learn when you see your family from an adult perspective.

Make a plan.
When you set out to be more neutral about your family and to learn more about them, always think through your goals for each visit.

Start small.
Don't go home with a barrage of questions. A first step in some families might be to go home and not give advice or try to change anyone. On a second visit you might ask one simple question about something you are curious about.

Use your level of anxiety as a guide.
Shifting your position in your family, or even beginning to become more neutral, will cause stress. This is not necessarily bad; it may be a sign you are on the right track. Simply begin to notice what happens: does your breathing get tight? Does your heart beat faster?

Breathe!
If you find yourself getting anxious, take some deep breaths. Oxygen will help your brain work better.

Take the long view.
Learning about our families and becoming more neutral about them is a lifelong process. We never complete our work on ourselves in relating to our families.

Celebrate your family heritage.
Be grateful for the strengths and the growing edge that are alive in your own experience.

There is no quick fix for family issues, but we can all experience gradual, slow growth if we want to work on it. Jon Kabat-Zinn suggests in *Coming to Our Senses,* "Family is usually such a wonderful laboratory for honing greater awareness, compassion, and wisdom, and actually embodying them in our everyday lives." Relating to our family from an adult perspective rather than the childish one we internalized when we were young is a big experiment. Our own family does become a laboratory for our own growth. The impact on our ministry may surprise us. And connecting with our families in a new way can actually be a spiritual practice in itself. (See chapter ten for more on this.)

One way to "honor your father and your mother" is to respect the multigenerational process that made them the people they are, with all their strengths and limitations. As Edwin Friedman said in *Generation to Generation,* "The problem with parents, after all, is that they had parents." Even the worst parts of our family story are part of the multigenerational process, and did not start with us or our parents.

❧ QUESTIONS TO PONDER

The patterns and processes of growing up in our particular family have a profound impact on our leadership. When we can begin to view our family differently, seeing them with adult eyes, we become better leaders. When we can recognize they did the best they could with what they were given (which may have been very limited indeed), we will be able to view them with more compassion and less judgment. The greatest gift we can give to those we lead, not to mention to ourselves and our children, is this kind of emotional freedom and flexibility. The effort is tremendous, but the payoff in every area of our lives is likewise enormous. We will automatically be better leaders when we learn to relate to our family of origin with more neutrality, with a greater repertoire of response, and with compassion. We will be better able to let go of the outcome of our leadership, yet at the same time be clearer about our purpose.

Here are seven questions to consider as you look at your family story:

- ❧ Who are the "good guys" and "bad guys"?

- ❧ Who are the matriarchs and patriarchs?

- ❧ Who are the family members no one speaks to? Or speaks about?

- ❧ Where are the divorces, the emotional and physical illnesses?

- ❧ What kind of work did people in my family do?

- ❧ When did parts of the family move away geographically?

- ❧ Where is the place of faith in the family?

CHAPTER 5

THINK IN THREES:

TRIANGLES AND LEADERSHIP

David taps on Susan's door. Susan is the new minister and is still getting to know the staff, while David is a long-time associate minister, and helps to plan worship. "Can I have a minute of your time?" he says. "I'd like to talk to you about Robert. I've got concerns about him." Robert is the music director, with an equally long tenure. Susan has already picked up the tension between the two, and she feels her heart begin to pound even before David launches into his complaints.

Why do leaders experience so much stress? One reason is this: we get caught in emotional triangles just like this one. But when we begin to understand how triangles work in organizations, we will know better which relationships we can affect and which are beyond our control. Learning to see triangles is the best stress-management tool around. It also helps make sense of the perplexing dynamics of relationships in congregational life.

To recognize emotional triangles we have to understand what they are. Psychiatrist Murray Bowen articulated the concept in order to describe the patterns he saw in the families he was studying. He noted that when the relationship between two people becomes troubled, they will pull in a third person as a way of achieving stability. Two squabbling children cry, "Mom!" An unhappy wife talks to her sister about her husband. A frustrated minister calls a colleague to let off steam about a difficult church member. Anxiety decreases, and the relationship is stabilized, for the time being.

Just as a two-legged stool is unstable and needs the third leg for balance, so also a two-person relationship is inherently unstable. The third person helps balance the relationship between the two. Some of the conflict between the first two (Person A and Person B) shifts into the relationship between Person B and the third person, C. In effect, Person C absorbs some of the 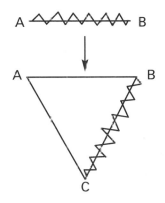 anxiety. The relationship between A and B can then calm down. This illustration shows how the tension (the jagged lines) moves from one relationship to the other when the triangle forms.

✎ FAMILY TRIANGLES

Triangles become particularly hard to deal with when they replicate intense triangles from our family of origin. When a crisis arises at church and you just can't see straight, it's time to take a look at the triangles, especially the ones in your own family. For example, if you were left out of a key decision about the new building, you may find your heart pounding and your body flooded with adrenaline. Rather than immediately asserting your authority, think about some family triangles in the past where you were left out while others were close to each other. You can find it useful to have a skilled coach or knowledgeable colleague to help, because you are so close to these hot triangles that it can be difficult to isolate them. In Susan's case, if she spent her childhood managing

two squabbling younger brothers, she may find herself reacting to David and Robert's difficulty in getting along more as
annoyed older sister than as senior minister.

Psychotherapist Elaine Boomer speaks of a "monster triangle" that tends to govern our interpersonal dealings. We all
have a triangle like this, usually with our mother and father.
Boomer says she gave it this name "because that triangle is so
powerful in functioning: it sets the parameters for how we're
going to function in close relationships. . . . It doesn't stand
alone, it's related to past generations. It's formed because parents come from families that have their own emotional
process."

For example, Boomer describes her own experience in a
triangle where she was very close to her father and distant
from her mother. She says she learned early that "you don't
cut your ties with your father, because you think that's all
you've got." She describes the way that plays out in adult relationships, where she finds herself more likely to give men
than women a decent break. And the triangle had its origins
in previous generations: her mother's mother was even more
distant in relationships.

Boomer worked with one pastor who grew up in a triangle where he was very distant from both parents. He felt a
lot of responsibility in relating to both parents, and that sense
of responsibility carries over into his ministry in ways that
cost him a lot. His parents also kept family secrets from him,
especially those about people who were having trouble with
life. He finds it hard to share with others the difficulties he is
having in his ministry. The isolation and burdens of the
"monster triangle" he grew up with are present in his leadership today.

The fundamental triangles from our families seem so
automatic to us that we will find it hard to step back and
assess them. We need time and perspective to be able to see
triangles: months, even years. And we can still easily get
caught in them. My automatic response is to take responsi-

bility, as a good oldest daughter of an oldest daughter who was also a pastor's daughter. I can find myself in a triangle with someone who appears the most responsible against another person who appears less responsible: "If we just get ourselves together we can whip this slacker into shape." This approach is rarely effective.

The greater our awareness of old family triangles, the better we will be able to manage ourselves. The moments when we cannot think straight become opportunities. The more intense the situation, the harder it is to see the triangles—and the bigger the payoff when we can get neutral enough to see them. We are in a lifelong process of self-awareness and learning. As we develop the ability to see triangles, we will automatically become less stressed and be more effective as leaders. Our energy will not be sapped trying to will what cannot be willed: people's relationships with others. Rather, we can begin to spend our energy on areas where we actually have control: our own thinking about the ministry, our self-management, and the relationships we have with others.[7]

Triangles first originate within the family, but they occur wherever people organize together. They can be seen everywhere in church life. For example, the pastor of a Baptist church makes a comment that the congregation president does not like, and the president complains to the vice president. A triangle is created: pastor – president – vice president. The music director at the Lutheran church chooses an anthem the choir hates, and a choir member gripes to her husband. Here is another triangle: music director – choir member – husband. The associate priest in an Episcopal church calls the senior warden to process an argument he just had with the parish secretary: priest – senior warden – secretary. The one forming the triangle feels better. In the case of the choir member complaining to her husband, she has let off steam; she has transferred some of her anxiety to her husband. However, chances are he feels worse. The greater his sense of responsibility for the relationship between the other two, the worse he feels, and the more stressed he becomes. If, for example, he chairs the music committee, he will feel a stronger responsibility to help the music director make the choir happy.

In pastoral care, triangles appear constantly. A worried mother consults with the youth minister about her teenage son. A daughter calls the pastor because she is concerned her mother is not eating right. Two family members planning a funeral each speak privately with the priest about the other. Triangles occur in all the families we work with, and in our own families.

Triangles are nothing new and we even have examples in the Bible, beginning with Adam. After Adam and Eve disobey God's command, Adam says to God, "The woman whom you gave to be with me, she gave me fruit from the tree" (Genesis 3:12). In the biblical story, Adam blames Eve to manage his anxiety over dealing directly with God. Blaming another person is one way you may form a triangle with someone who is criticizing you. Another way is to ally with a partner for a common advantage, as when the disciples James and John ask Jesus for special treatment. Or you can pull in another party to make a decision you do not want to make, as when Pilate invites the crowd to decide whether he should free Jesus.

✎ MANAGING OURSELVES IN TRIANGLES

Leaders cannot stay out of triangles: they are a fact of life. Moreover, triangles are not necessarily bad—they are simply part of human experience. Yet how we manage ourselves within the triangles we face at church can make or break a pastoral encounter, or even our entire ministry.

We manage poorly within triangles when we function out of our own anxiety and take responsibility for the relationships of others. Taking responsibility for other people's relationships is one way we often overfunction. We feel anxious when others have difficulty relating, so we rush in to fix the problem. Another way we function poorly is automatically to take one person's side in a triangle. For example, when a parent comes to you to complain about the youth director, you exclaim, "That's terrible! We're going to have to do something about that," and immediately charge off, furious, to deal with the youth leader.

We can, however, learn to conduct ourselves more effectively in the triangles where we play a part. We can learn to recognize the triangles we are part of, and to respond less automatically ("That's terrible!") and more thoughtfully ("Let me think about what to do next").

Here is a situation that clergy face over and over. One long-time church member becomes disgruntled with the new minister and invites a number of members over for coffee, one after another, to review her list of complaints. By doing this she creates a number of triangles with the minister and each of these members, and the consequences can be disastrous for him and for the church. When the minister realizes what is going on, he panics—is this the end of his ministry? But if he calms down, works out a strategy, and contacts her directly as well as touching base with the other members, he will be able to manage his automatic defensive response. So instead of spiraling into conflict, the simmering discontent subsides; the woman leaves the congregation but the minister keeps his job and can move forward. Triangles tend to arise at times of heightened anxiety, but if we can notice what is going on, stay calm, and stay in touch with the people involved, a better outcome is likely.

❧ KEYS TO TRIANGLES

As you begin to recognize the triangles around you, you can make choices about how to relate to people within them. Here are five keys to understanding triangles and how to approach them.

1) You cannot change the other side of a triangle.
In other words, you cannot change a relationship you do not belong to. In Susan's triangle with David and Robert, she cannot directly affect their relationship. It does not matter whether the other two people in the triangle are staff members, as in this case, two members of the council or vestry, or your spouse and a church member. Their relationship is their responsibility, not yours. The way you relate to each of them individually has the potential to shift the way they relate to each other, but you cannot make the change directly. If someone complains to you about another person in the congregation, there is nothing you can do to change or improve their relationship. Simply letting go of that responsibility will spare you a lot of unnecessary stress.

2) If you try to change the other side of a triangle, the situation often gets worse.
This is not a conscious phenomenon (as in, "We're going to get back at him for trying to change us!"), but an automatic reaction. People resist willful attempts to change them. The more Susan anxiously tries to help David and Robert get along, the more they will be in conflict. Or, in another scenario, the more she tries to reduce David's dependency on Robert, the more dependent David will become. People automatically resist our efforts to rearrange their relationships. They are not necessarily intentionally defying us. Recall in chapter two we talked about homeostasis, or balance. The system of human relationships tends to keep the balance it has already achieved.

When you are more motivated for people to change than they are, then you have a problem—and they have all the power. The more they resist, the more you get sucked in. The more energy you spend trying to change them, the more things stay the same. This is equally true in a marriage, in parenting, or in leading a choir, a church, a judicatory, or a denomination.

3) When you try to change someone else's relationship, you carry the stress that belongs to the other two.

Trying to do the impossible always creates stress. David and Robert will be relieved as a result of Susan's efforts to reconcile them because they will experience less stress: she has taken on what belongs to them. But there is also no potential for change.

When my children were in elementary school, they often came crying to me to help them get along with each other. I spent a lot of energy trying to fix their relationship. The result of my effort was that I became worn out and the children kept fighting. Finally, I decided to take less responsibility for whether they got along or not; I worked on managing my own responses and on being less invested in their relationship. Sometimes I would define myself to them: "I'm not going to listen to this any more—I've got other things to do right now"; or, "If you are going to argue, please go upstairs." Paradoxically, I found that the less intense my interactions with them became, the better they got along.

4) You can change a relationship you belong to.

You can directly influence your own relationship with each of the other two in a triangle. You can change that relationship because you are part of it. Making this change can shift the other relationship between them, but once again, you cannot affect that directly. Susan can make sure she is well-connected to David but also stays in touch with Robert. If she is present in the triangle with them in a clear but non-willful way, there is potential for change. Since she supervises them both, for example, she can say to them, "You can't have loud arguments with each other in the church building if you want to keep working here."

In my example of a quarrel between a choir member and the choir director, you can coach them to talk to each other. You can ask neutral questions to help them think more clearly. Most important, as you let go emotionally of whether or not they get along, their relationship is likely to improve.

The most important stance in a triangle is to be as neutral as possible in relating to the two others. This does not necessarily mean that you do not have a position on the issue at hand. Maybe you think the choice of the anthem was not appropriate, or you just did not like it either. But you are not taking emotional responsibility for how they relate to each other, which is something quite different from the content or apparent cause of the tension. The specifics of what you say are less important than maintaining emotional neutrality. This means you can stay in contact with both sides, while staying out of people's attempts to get you emotionally on their side.[8] When you get caught up in the emotional field of other people's relationships, you lose your ability to be of real help to them. Challenging others to be more adult in their relationships is in everyone's best interests.

5) Finally, triangles interlock, and occur over generations.
For example, I once heard a man claim that his father favored him over his older sister and everyone knew it. He described the pressures this put on him as well as his sister. In the next moment I heard him say, "Good job, Steven!" to his son while ignoring his older daughter's attempts to get his attention. The triangle continued in the next generation. Clergy become part of these complex triangles when we are called in to help pastorally. One classic eternal triangle involves a husband, his mistress, and his wife. This triangle becomes a set of interlocking triangles when the wife calls the pastor for help.

Triangles also recur over time in congregational life. If David and Robert are causing problems at church by the conflicted nature of their relationship, Susan might undertake a research project. Where else in the church are there similar relationships? Are their jobs "trouble spots" historically? One congregation was polarized over its new pastor (a common triangle in churches is that of pastor–supporters–opponents). Church leaders found that the same pattern had occurred twice in quick succession a generation earlier. The long tenure of a beloved pastor in recent years meant people had forgotten the earlier conflict, but the triangle persisted.

☜ MOVEMENT WITHIN TRIANGLES

Typically, in triangles two people are closer, while the third person is on the outside. When tension arises between the two who are close, one of them will move to the outside as the second allies with the third. If Susan takes a stand with David and Robert and insists they behave differently, they may find themselves shifting closer to each other, and commiserating about the overly tough new minister.

In one congregation John (the rector) and Elizabeth (the senior warden) may be very close, while Steve (the junior warden) does his part but is not that close to either one. Then Elizabeth decides that the rector has not been attentive enough to her husband when he was in the hospital; she begins to complain to Steve, and suddenly John is on the outside of the triangle. You can map anxiety in a congregation (or a family) by watching the movement of people in and out of triangles—the alliances they form, who is on the inside, and who is on the outside.

As you learn to understand triangles you also begin to see the character of the relationships within them. For example, look for conflict between two of the parties to a triangle. Assess the emotional distance between one of those people and the third person. When people are very close the relationship can be problematic because the two may be too dependent on each other to grow. The patterns may be the same over time, or the conflict / distance / closeness may move around the triangle to the different relationships. In healthier systems, relationships are not rigidly fixed. Movement in relationships can allow room for growth.

The following illustration shows how tension or conflict can move from one side of the triangle to another.

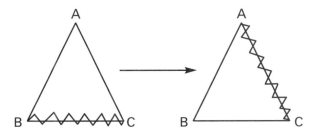

When the triangles are fixed, patterns repeat themselves and there is less opportunity for new learning. To go back to an earlier example, there may be a constant battle between the music director and the associate minister, with the senior minister mediating, that can go on for years. Somehow this pattern seems to happen over and over, no matter who occupies the positions. Every church has these patterns, but some are more fixed than others. The recurring relationship challenge gets in the way of moving toward ministry goals. Furthermore, when you think only in terms of individuals, you may make the mistake of assuming that if you simply change the personnel, the problem goes away. When you think systemically, you know these ongoing patterns are much deeper than that, and are embedded in the emotional life of the organization itself. Even if the conflict is intense for a short time, when triangles are not locked in one place, that is a sign of greater health. When relationships are more flexible, people tend to be more mature, and have more options in facing life challenges.

☙ TRIANGLES IN CONGREGATIONS

The best way for leaders to manage triangles is always self-management. Stepping back to examine the triangles gives you some distance, some perspective. While you may be passionately involved with your work, you also need to step back and get a broader view. Ronald Heifetz, in *Leadership without Easy Answers,* uses the image of the balcony at a dance. You have to go up onto the balcony in order to see the patterns of the dancers. When you get some distance from the emotional patterns in the church, you will be able to see the triangles more clearly and manage yourself in relation to them.

When you learn to see triangles, you can begin to make sense of puzzling behavior in congregational life. When people behave in confusing ways, there may be a triangle involved. For example, a church member begins to distance himself from the church for no apparent reason. You may discover later that he has begun to reconcile with his estranged wife—and the church has come to be on the outside of that triangle. You cannot always know all the parties to a triangle. But recognizing their existence can help manage your own anxiety and depersonalize the situation. You quit wondering, "Why are they doing this to me?" and wonder, rather, "What might be going on here?"

Looking for triangles is one way to get perspective. You can also be a researcher or anthropologist of your institution. What patterns do you observe? Looking for triangles and other recurring relationships may make inexplicable phenomena understandable. As a result, your own anxiety will decrease, and you will be better able to think clearly and decide on your own next steps.

In a time of turmoil in church life, try this exercise. Sit down and diagram the triangles you see, and where you are positioned in them—where is the conflict, the distance, and the over-closeness? If you are in the middle of a lot of triangles, you may realize why you feel so stressed. This exercise is a way to get a little distance from the intensity, which is a step toward being more neutral about the whole situation. Every time I plot the triangles in an intense situation, I can feel myself beginning to calm down. The exercise helps me see where I am caught, and to see some additional choices in how I can relate to others.

As we saw in chapter two, your primary responsibilities are to manage yourself and the part you play in relationships with others. When you remember this, you can better negotiate the triangles in which you live and work. Your anxiety will be lower, and a thoughtful response will be more likely. For example, rather than feeling left out when you find yourself on the outside of a triangle, you can strategize to work on your relationship with each individual. When Susan notices David and Robert moving closer to each other and away from her, she can make a point of connecting with each one of them separately. She might try to have some lighthearted conversations with each to develop the connection, rather than a heavy-handed supervisory session.

In the case of the rector in a triangle with the two wardens, he might have coffee with each individually. The purpose would be not to process the situation, but simply to spend time together or to talk about church goals. The content of the disagreement is not the most important thing, but how the rector makes a connection with each one.

Creating a triangle is not always a bad thing to do. You can strategically bring others into a triangle as a leadership move. For example, if a church member is persistently hostile, you may want to ally yourself with the congregation president to help address the situation. If the church is facing a financial crisis, leaders need to know. At some point the congregation needs to be brought in. There is a big difference between anxiously pulling others into a triangle and thoughtfully considering who legitimately shares responsibility for the difficulties at hand. This is true both in the way you create the triangle and in the ultimate outcome. Anxiously created triangles lead to anxiety-driven results. Thoughtfully created triangles can help people become more creative about addressing challenges, and can place the responsibility where it belongs.

Triangles and New Ministries

Every pastor enters a congregation in a triangle with that congregation and his or her predecessor. If the predecessor was beloved, the new pastor comes in on the outside of a triangle. If the predecessor's ministry went badly and he or she was forced out, the opposite happens: the pastor gets drawn in close with the congregation. Church members want the current pastor to be on their side against the terrible behavior of that other pastor.

Once again, the key is to be as neutral as possible. You will not win trying to make yourself look better than your wonderful predecessor. Nor will you win by ganging up on the guy who had to go. Church members will try to draw you into these triangles. When you get caught up with them, you are only perpetuating the intensity of the past. In both cases, the better approach is to work on yourself so you are indeed as neutral as possible: not defensive in relation to a beloved predecessor or smug in relation to a perceived failure. Triangles with the preceding leader are the most intense after the retirement of a long-term pastor or when you follow a pastor who engaged in misconduct of some kind. Still, they are present at the beginning of any new ministry.

TRIANGLES AND ANXIETY

Pay attention to triangles that develop during congregational conversations about important issues and decisions. When you are convinced you know the right direction to go, it is all too easy to form triangles, with people who agree with you on the inside and those who disagree on the outside. Whether the issue is a new building program, a change in worship, a new mission direction, or hiring new staff, you can watch the process at work. Even when you have a strong opinion, you can still stay neutral in relationship with others. You can make an effort to stay connected to those who disagree with you, rather than taking the easy way out and staying distant from them. Remaining connected is pastorally and strategically the right thing to do. The best ministry takes place over a long period of time, and building relationships even with those who disagree most strongly will pay off later.

At times of anxiety, such as periods of decision-making or conflict, people form even more triangles, with more whispered conversations by the coffee pot and more meetings in the church parking lot. People who are upset with you may leave you on the outside of the information loop. You can observe this without getting too paranoid about it. The fact is, even when people really are out to get you, the leader's response can make a difference to the outcome. It is easy to get defensive when we are on the outside of a lot of triangles, but responding anxiously rarely helps. Holding a lighter, more curious attitude—"There they go again!" or, "I wonder what's coming next!"—can help lower your own anxiety and that of other leaders.

One way to function at times of high anxiety is to be a conduit of information, and to refuse to keep secrets. Secrets create triangles, with the insiders knowing the secret and the outside person or group not knowing, at least not con-sciously. When you think systemically, you begin to under-stand that the system knows all the secrets anyway. Children know something is not quite right with their parents, no mat-ter how much parents try to protect them. In the same way, people in a congregation sense something is going on even when they do not know what it is. In times of higher anxi-ety it is better to be as open as possible.

The least mature people in a congregation are masters at sucking others into triangles. Whether a mother wants you to help shape up her troubled son or a worshipper wants you to be his ally against others who want different music in wor-ship, it is easy to be infected by their anxiety. In fact, you can use this to assess how mature people are: how able are they to speak directly to others, or how prone are they to create triangles ("Don't tell Sally, but . . .")?

So what are you to do, if you cannot change the other side of a triangle? You work on the relationships of which you are a part. You try to have direct, one-to-one relationships, especially with staff and key leaders in the congregation. You develop a wider perspective on what is going on by mapping out triangles and potential triangles. Taking the time for a diagram on paper is always worth it. You let go of the responsibility for other people's relationships and take responsibility for your own relationships.

➷ PASTORAL TRIANGLES

Dr. Lawrence Matthews uses the phrase "pastoral triangle" to describe a triangle that involves the pastor, the church he or she leads, and the pastor's vision of the ideal church. When the pastor is imposing his or her will by insisting that the church become this "ideal," resistance and the resulting stress are inevitable. People resist being coerced—even in the service of a compelling vision.

Matthews points out that the leader has power in relation to the church and in relation to the vision, because of the direct connection. The leader can and must connect to, relate to, and challenge the group in order to exert influence. "The leader can address the vision or goal in several ways: define self, interpret and teach biblical concepts, clarify his or her understanding of the goals," he says. "To the extent that the pastor (A) assumes responsibility for the B–C side of the triangle, A

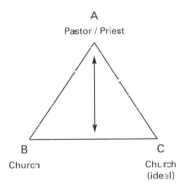

THE PASTORAL TRIANGLE

A
Pastor / Priest

B
Church

C
Church
(ideal)

will experience the stress and emotional kickback that belongs between B and C." He then quotes Friedman, saying,

"Stress comes from taking responsibility that rightfully belongs to (and therefore can only be assumed by) others." When a pastor takes responsibility for a relationship he or she does not belong to, the church's relationship with its identity and future, burnout can result.

A less stressful approach is to relate as fully as we can to the church we do have, and define as clearly as we can our vision of the ideal church. When we put the vision out there, without overly high expectations of how the church will relate to the vision, there is room for conversation, and for people to make a choice. It is hard work to relate to both sides of the pastoral triangle—but not impossible. Making a church into God's church is impossible, and it is not our job, anyway— that is up to God.

☙ QUESTIONS TO PONDER

Triangles are part of human experience, even part of creation. Luke tells this story: "Someone in the crowd said to Jesus, 'Teacher, tell my brother to divide the family inheritance with me.' But he said to him, 'Friend, who set me to be a judge or arbitrator over you?'" (Luke 12:13–14). When we, like Jesus in this story, can see triangles for what they are, and get less caught up in them, we will have more energy for ministry. We will be better able to challenge others to grow, and to grow up. We will find ourselves able to be clearer about our own goals, rather than getting caught up in goals for others that they may not share. And when we enter into the most challenging times of ministry, we will find our ability to persist enhanced by the wider perspective we have gained.

Here are seven questions about triangles for you to think about:

- What are the triangles in this particular pastoral situation?

- What relationships am I taking responsibility for?

64

- Where am I feeling left out because I am on the outside of a triangle?

- Who is bringing me into a triangle to manage his or her own anxiety?

- Which of my own "old buttons" are being pushed?

- How will I choose to relate to the other people in this triangle, rather than taking my automatic position?

- What can I learn about myself in this triangle?

CHAPTER 6

KNOW YOUR

PURPOSE

When Rabbi Noah, Rabbi Mordecai's son, assumed the succession after his father's death, his disciples noticed that there
were a number of ways in which he conducted himself differently than his father, and asked him about this. "I do just
as my father did," Rabbi Noah replied. "He did not imitate,
and I do not imitate."[9]

Fundamentally, leadership is having a clear sense of who
we are and where we are going, and relating to our followers out of ourselves. The best leaders are themselves in
their role, rather than imitating other leaders or looking to
their followers for their primary cues. They know who they
are and what their purpose is.

In our culture we focus a lot of attention on the personality of leaders and on leadership style, but personality, style,
and technique do not determine success. For example, two
football coaches, Vince Lombardi of the Green Bay Packers
and Tom Landry of the Dallas Cowboys, were nearly opposite in temperament. Lombardi was fiery and never hesitated
to chew out his players when they were not performing. He
immediately turned around a failing team, and became a leg-

end. Landry was reserved and undemonstrative, deeply religious, and extremely low-key. Like Lombardi, he also got results, with twenty consecutive winning seasons—a record that still stands a generation later. Simply imitating either of their styles, as many coaches have, has not guaranteed the same outcome.

In the same way, different styles of ministry can be effective. One clergy leader might be tough, like Lombardi, almost aggressive in style, constantly offering challenges to the congregation. The result can be a ministry that is growing and thriving, despite what some might see as a style that is too edgy for church. Another leader can be quiet and reserved, like Landry, yet consistent and clear in communicating his or her leadership message. The quiet leadership presence can also get results.

Clergy might try to imitate either of these two ministers to try to get the same outcome—a thriving ministry. Yet the point is not that each of them has done ministry in a certain style, but rather that they both have done ministry in a style that fits them. They have learned who they are, and rather than developing a certain technique of ministry or following a particular model, they have found a way to do the work that is comfortable for them. When we look for the right leadership style, the place to look is within ourselves. The more we find our own rhythm of leadership, the better off we will be. We will be able to sustain ourselves for a long time when we are leading in a way that is true to ourselves because we will not be wasting energy trying to be someone else.

Vince Lombardi understood this. Sonny Jurgensen, who played one season under Lombardi as quarterback for the Redskins in 1969, told this story:

> Coach Lombardi called me into his office once he got
> settled in, and his first words to me were, "I've heard a
> lot of things about you as a person and as a player, and
> I'm sure you've heard a lot of things about me. Well,
> that's got nothing to do with our relationship. I just

ask one thing of you: I want you to be yourself. Don't emulate anyone else. Don't try to be someone you're not. Just be yourself."[10]

Mature leaders know that imitating others is no answer. They know how they function in their own work and in dealing with others. They are clear on where they are headed, and they can persist through the ups and downs of life. Knowing our leadership purpose becomes a lifetime endeavor. For church leaders it is a spiritual endeavor as well, involving prayer and discernment. Who has God made you to be, and how is God calling you to lead?

☙ FINDING YOUR PURPOSE

Finding your purpose is not a to-do item you can complete and check off the list, but an ongoing process of discernment. Purpose involves more than one level of our life and work. It includes big questions such as: What am I on this planet for? Who am I, and what are my best gifts? And it also involves some shorter term questions: What is my purpose in my role in this ministry? Where am I headed right now, and what do I need to do to get there? Beginning to develop some answers to the bigger questions will help make the more immediate questions easier to answer. Our consideration of these questions may include thinking about theology, the traditions of the church, new models of ministry, appropriate worship styles, and practical questions such as how to fund our ministry dream. I would like to suggest five elements that I think are important.

1) Spending time alone.

For the many extraverts in pastoral ministry this can be difficult. But the reality is that no one else can tell you who you are or what your purpose is, except God. We simply need to find time apart to think clearly. Leaders who are always too busy for a time of quiet reflection are probably too close to the action to have a clear perspective. Physical distance is not everything; we need emotional distance as well. Still, getting out of town can help. Part of knowing yourself is knowing how you work best, and what contributes to your best thinking about your purpose.

2) Doing family of origin work.
As I described this work earlier in chapter four, learning more about where we came from and engaging with our families in a more neutral way will help us know our purpose more clearly. Our families gave us our first teaching on what our purpose should be, and working on difficult family of origin issues can help us claim our adult purpose.

3) Putting your purpose into practice.
Taking some small steps toward what you feel most drawn to can help clarify your sense of purpose. It is a process that we are in, but we can wake up a bit more each day. Every day, put on your to-do list something that gives you joy. Include one ministry task that gives you joy and one personal activity that gives you joy. For example, if you love to study, read part of an article every day. If you love nature, spend at least a little time outside every day. Becoming ourselves in our ministry involves finding hope and joy, not simply grim determination and a sense of obligation. Keep yourself in a creative space in ministry, and even allow yourself to do something new badly, to see if you like it.

4) Finding appropriate support.
We all need help with discernment, whether it is from a spiritual director, coach, therapist, mentor, or mature colleague. No one can tell us who we are, but having someone in our lives who can ask good questions to help us discern who we are and what we are after can be useful. I recommend it. Many clergy are in support groups, and in choosing one to join I think it is important to discern the nature of the group: a gripe session will not help you. Yet a group that can chal-

lenge you to be thoughtful about yourself and your ministry may indeed be useful.

5) Practicing patience.
Clarity of purpose has to emerge from within, and that takes time. We have to spend time thinking about our purpose, and we have to allow time to elapse before the purpose emerges. As Lao-Tzu asked, "Do you have the patience to wait till your mud settles and the water is clear? Can you remain unmoving till the right action arises by itself?"[11] There are always new pebbles thrown into the pond, and we must pause anew from time to time. We will find our clarity evolves over time.

ꙮ Maintaining Your Purpose

This kind of maturity never happens in isolation; a key element is our connection with others. It is easy for us to know our purpose when we are all alone, but what happens when we enter the pulpit or the board meeting, or even sit down at the family dinner table? Leadership involves managing the delicate balance between individuality (knowing our own clear purpose) and togetherness (managing our relationships with those we lead). This is true for all leaders, from the family house to the White House. And as we get clear, others will respond. An old saying goes, "If it's foggy in the pulpit, it's damned cloudy in the pews."

Edwin Friedman talked about leadership through self-differentiation, which he described this way:

> It refers to a direction in life rather than a state of being, to the capacity to take a stand in an intense emotional system, to saying "I" when others are demanding "we,"... to maintaining a non-anxious presence in the face of anxious others. [12]

When we look to others, whether they be other leaders or our own followers, as our primary guides, we are borrowing our purpose from them, rather than looking within or to

God. We borrow our purpose from others when the denomination suggests a program or goal and we sign on for it because we are a loyalist. We borrow our purpose when we say to our followers, "Where do you want to go? I'll lead you there." Others will always be glad to tell us what our purpose is and who we ought to be, so that our purpose becomes serving other people's agendas. All too often we want our congregations to do well not for their sake but for our own, to make us feel good about ourselves and to look good to others.

A borrowed purpose is not a purpose that will last. When we know our identity and direction, we can find greater stamina and the ability to carry on, even when things get difficult. If we live out of our own purpose a bit more each day, we will find greater energy and satisfaction in our ministry. Parker Palmer talks about the nature of vocation. The word *vocation* is rooted in the Latin for "voice." Palmer says, "Vocation does not come from a voice 'out there' calling me to become something I am not. It comes from a voice 'in here' calling me to be the person I was born to be, to fulfill the original selfhood given me at birth by God."[13] As Rabbi Noah said, "He did not imitate, and I do not imitate." The less we imitate, the greater the power our leadership has.

It is in relationship that we learn how to balance persistence with the need to adapt. Yes, we need to pursue our purpose, but that does not mean we get everything we want. We can have our ears open to listen for the response we get, and if people know we are open to hearing what they have to say, and that we will adapt as necessary along the way, our message will get a better reception. So we pursue our purpose authentically and persistently but not stubbornly or inflexibly.

And the paradox of growth is this: as we become more mature, our repertoire of responses broadens and matures, which can lead to some new ways of leading. I once told a close colleague, "I don't do conflict!" But over time, I have learned to deal with conflict and take a firm stand when necessary; it has added something new to my repertoire. If we tend to be passive, we may need to take more initiative. If we are naturally very serious, we may need to lighten up a bit.

∾ VOICING YOUR PURPOSE

Finding your own voice means learning to say "I"—"I believe," "Here I stand," "I will do this," "I won't do that." Saying "I," defining self, requires both strength and maturity. There are always pressures to conform: attend a meeting of any church or denominational group, no matter what the ecclesiology or theology, and watch people recruiting others for their position.

I often hear the clergy I coach saying something very clear about their hopes and dreams for their ministry. When I ask them, "Have you said that to your congregation?" almost inevitably the answer comes, "Well, not in so many words." Leadership means we need to go out on a limb and actually tell those we lead where we want to go. The fear is, of course, that if we say what we really want, we may not get it. But if we never say it, we definitely will not get it. We are never guaranteed success, and God does not require it of us. Still, stepping out to articulate our purpose and direction is an essential component of leadership.

Of course, we take into consideration the views of others, and clearly pursuing our goals does not mean we run roughshod over everyone else. The Reverend J. Edwin Bacon, Jr., rector of All Saints Episcopal Church in Pasadena, California, describes the leadership process this way: "It starts with being clear about where you end and somebody else begins. You get clear about what you believe, and express that in a differentiated and inviting way." The purpose comes from within, and is shared with others. As important as it is to know our purpose, leadership only occurs when we actually speak about our purpose to others who can then choose to follow.

So, think through how to share it. Articulating our purpose to our followers must always go along with letting go of the outcome, and with an ongoing effort to build relationships. Finding our voice means that we say, steadily and over time, what our most important principles are and where we are going, inviting others to come along. Make a plan for what you want to say and when and how to say it. And remember these words from Luke's gospel: "No one after lighting a lamp hides it under a jar, or puts it under a bed, but puts it on a lampstand, so that those who enter may see the light" (8:16). The same is true for you in articulating your purpose.

It is certainly true that taking a stand in the moment is always a risk, and can make us uncomfortable. Finding our voice as a leader can feel wrong at first. And we can feel tremendous internal discomfort when we discern a new purpose for ourselves and begin to live it out, by saying "I" amid intense pressure to say "we." Others can respond with disapproval and even anger. In some churches, suggesting a new direction is nearly heresy. When we do not conform to the expected patterns, we can feel out of control. Yet if we stick with it, living and leading out of our real purpose becomes more natural. Other people come to terms with our stance, whether or not they agree.

Here are seven questions to ask yourself as you strive to achieve clarity in your vocation:

- Where do I want to go?

- What energizes me?

- What future possibilities do I see?

- What legacy do I want to leave?

- Do I know what I love to do? Can I do more of it?

- What was my original thinking in going into ministry?

- If I had to write down my ministry purpose in one sentence right this minute, what would I say?

❧ THE PROBLEM OF WILLFULNESS

The Reverend Cynthia Maybeck of Northborough, Massachusetts, wanted to introduce a time of prayer and spiritual formation at the regular deacons' meeting, which had previously been focused only on church business. At first this suggestion was not popular, and one of the deacons asked every meeting for months, "Do we really have to do this spiritual stuff?" Maybeck was very clear from the beginning what she wanted, yet she gave them time to come along and recognized it was their choice to do so. Now, she says, "They are the ones who ask the 'spiritual' questions instead of my always having to do it." As a result, in a recent budget crisis at the church the deacons themselves framed that challenge in spiritual terms, not simply financial ones. This was not an overnight process, however; it took years.

Lao-Tzu asks, "Can you love people and lead them without imposing your will?"[14] Is it possible to be fully engaged in the process of leadership while still holding the outcome lightly? Willfulness is the relentless pursuit of our goals without regard for the opinions or discernment of others. It is trying hard to enlist others to our point of view rather than articulating our vision clearly and giving them time and space. We are willful when we only listen to others long enough to figure out how to refute their argument. And after a while, we begin to view others as a means to an end, as tools to help us reach our goals, or as obstacles in the way.

In order for any group to move forward, the leader has to step out and say, "I'm going in this direction." People long for leadership. When a leader is clear, calm, and confident, people find their own confidence increased, and they are more likely to follow. They sense that they can trust this leader, that there is some substance to the course the leader is charting. This setting of a direction is a critical part of the role of leadership. Yet the trap for leaders can be that we find ourselves caught up with the goal we are pursuing. We spend a tremendous amount of energy cajoling and convincing people to follow the path we are on. We find ourselves being willful toward others. We cling to the outcomes we want, finding it all too easy to do everything we can to get everyone else to go along with us.

We can pursue many different kinds of ministry outcomes. We may be after a specific result: numbers in the pews, a stewardship goal, meeting the budget at the end of the year, having the staff get along, having the congregation vote for a capital campaign. An outcome may be something less definable, like the overall success of our ministry, or feeling like we have done a good job. Cynthia Maybeck wanted to have deacons who could be spiritual leaders in the congregation, not simply administrators and decision-makers.

There is a fine line between willfulness and pursuing a goal with energy and determination. Willfulness has more to do with the emotional energy we direct at others in trying to get them on board with our goals. Willfulness does not mean using our will in the energetic pursuit of our goals. That effort is essential for leaders; making a difference in the world does require serious commitment. You cannot lead a congregation if you do not care about ministry and the people in the church. Willfulness does mean we anxiously pressure others to agree with us and come along.

This happens for a number of reasons. First of all, we want to make a difference in ministry. We develop these dreams and plans and programs with the best of intentions, and often with some real knowledge about what makes ministry go well. We want to make *this* church into our vision of the ideal church. But we also cling to our goals out of fear: If I don't reach these ministry goals, who am I? If I'm not leading a numerically growing church, I'm a failure. If people don't sign up for my vision, they are rejecting me. We define our value by our results. We want someone to say, "Well done, good and faithful servant." Our identity is caught up in a powerful way with the outcome of our efforts. This often goes back to our family story, and how we received messages of why we were valued. We want to succeed, we want to look good, we want others to think well of us—in the community, in the denomination, and in our family.

We may believe our goal seems obvious: of course our worship needs to evolve to connect with the next generations. Or, obviously this philosophy of children's ministry has outlived its usefulness, and we have to find a new way. Or, of course our church structure is cumbersome and does not help us meet our needs. Why can't others see what seems self-evident to us?

Just as the person who desperately wants to be liked is never the most popular, the leader who desperately wants others to follow is not the most effective. This is true even when the stakes seem high. The more you chase them, the less likely they are to follow. Murray Bowen used to say, "You can't make a bean plant grow by pulling on it." In the same way, you cannot make people follow by pulling on them. Others will more readily persevere on a road freely chosen, especially when things get difficult.

When we will others to change, they resist change. People resent being willed to go in a certain direction, and they know instinctively when it is happening. Using our will on other human beings, rather than in the pursuit of our goals, often ends up being an invasion of boundaries. And just as a nation resists an invading army as powerfully as possible, so also people resist the invasion by another personality. Often all our efforts at convincing someone else of our point of view become our attempt to will them to agree with us. The message we give often does not invite real discussion. Larry Matthews suggests:

> Coercion is a basic ethical issue for leaders. It is my experience that leaders who are working at their own self-definition are better able to resist the temptation to will others into compliance with their ideas and goals. To focus upon clarifying and communicating one's

own ideas and goals is an invitation for others to do the same. [15]

From the outside, the difference between a leader who is taking a clear, self-defined stand and a leader who is being stubborn or autocratic may not be obvious. The leaders' words may even sound the same, but the emotional freight they carry is very different and the human response will be different. Autocratic leadership gets in the way of real progress because it permits only unquestioning agreement or automatic resistance, not mature conversation and decision-making. In addition, being an autocratic leader will wear you out. You can expend a tremendous amount of energy cheerleading, persuading, or coercing others. You spend more time trying to read people's minds than thinking about what you believe and are committed to.

The Reverend James Lamkin, pastor of Northside Drive Baptist Church in Atlanta, Georgia, says that he often fools himself into thinking he has outgrown the Serenity Prayer, originally composed by Reinhold Niebuhr:

God grant me the serenity
to accept the things I cannot change;
courage to change the things I can;
and wisdom to know the difference.

Lamkin suggests, "The serenity prayer is about willfulness. To accept the things I cannot change means I can't change history and I can't change other people. Then, the courage to change the things I *can* change means me." One of the gifts that his congregation has given him in twelve years is the realization that he cannot *will* the congregation into his goals, so his most important task is to focus on himself: his clarity, his own functioning as leader of the congregation. Over time, we all learn versions of this difficult lesson. We can learn it by beating our head against the wall, or we can begin to learn a humble acceptance of the limitations of our own leadership and of our role.

❧ FOCUS ON SELF

What does it mean to focus on ourselves and our own goals, as Lamkin suggests? Isn't it selfish to focus on self? In his book on leadership, Edwin Friedman asks how leaders are "to value, indeed treasure and preserve self without worrying that they are being narcissistic or autocratic. To resort to being only an 'enabler' for others or to try to concentrate on building teams instead simply fudges the issue. *Someone still has to go first!*"[16] Focusing on ourselves in this way is an essential part of our role: our followers need to know there is some substance to our leadership. It is not self-centered for leaders to know themselves and their own purposes; it is essential. We do our followers a disservice if we are not clear about where we would like to go. Having a clear sense of self as a leader is different from being an autocrat.

Leading while holding the outcome lightly does not mean you do not care whether the church makes progress, or you do not care where you are going. Instead, you offer a clear direction, all the while recognizing the ultimate outcome is beyond your control. Others must choose to come along. This kind of leadership is not passive; it requires active engagement and constant attention from the leader. But the attention is at least as much on ourselves and our own clarity, as well as tending to our inner life and managing how we react to others, as it is on whether people are following us or not.

Here is an example. Brian, a newly called pastor who is ready to chart a vision for the parish, wrote a clear statement of where he wanted to go, in particular his vision for community outreach, and began to think through a plan for sharing the vision with others. When he first broached the subject with the executive committee of the vestry, he was surprised by how hesitant they were. In fact, he was shocked, forgetting that *every* search committee says that the church wants to grow.

After this meeting, he realized it was too soon to bring these matters to the full council, so he brought the question again to the next executive committee meeting. After some coaching, he was in a different frame of mind. He realized that deciding to move in the direction of outreach was really not up to him. He could frame the discussion, and he could commit himself, but the executive committee had to make its own decision: he could not make that happen. So Brian disciplined himself to speak to them a different way, saying, "I think, I believe, I see," without saying, "we" or "you." Then he sat back in his chair and concentrated on breathing slowly and calmly. He began to notice that people were responding differently this time. At the end of the meeting, the moderator said, "I think we should talk about this with the council, and I'll recommend we consider moving in the direction Brian is suggesting."

What changed? Of course Brian used different language, and positioned himself a bit differently. But the big change was in him—the shift that came about through recognizing he could not control the outcome of this decision. He did not take their concerns as a personal affront, but recognized it was going to take some time for people to come along, to get their questions answered, and to decide for themselves what they thought about this new direction for the church's ministry. Brian is likely to encounter more setbacks along the way toward his goals; he will have months and years of hard work, planning, and implementing, putting in the time to relate to key leaders in the congregation, taking a step back when an element of the program has to be retooled, licking his wounds when the inevitable pushback comes from congregational members. He will need endless reserves of patience, and he will need to keep his vision in mind throughout—and will need to adapt and adjust the vision along the way in response to the feedback he gets.

The principle is the same all along the way: leaders need to continue to define themselves and their goals. This is the most important task of leadership, whether you are leading a small congregation or an entire denomination.

A classic example of self-definition by a leader is Martin Luther King, Jr., in his August 28, 1963, speech at the Lincoln Memorial: "I have a dream that one day on the red hills of Georgia, the sons of former slaves and the sons of former slave owners will be able to sit down together at the table of brotherhood." He never says, "You did," "You ought," or "You should." He simply says, "I have a dream." The Reverend Michael Nel, director of the Lutheran Consultation to Clergy, remembers hearing King's speech as a twenty-two-year-old white man in South Africa. "His self-definition made it very powerful. It rang across the world. When you are living in a country where you don't think a new future is possible, in the midst of the intensity of the racism, to hear that is unique.... His approach influenced my preaching afterwards, because I think preaching *is* self-definition."

Similarly, Jesus is always more focused on his own message and mission than on whether anyone decides to follow him. Jesus more often says, "I." In the Sermon on the Mount, he says, "You have heard it said, ... but I say to you." In the gospel of John, Jesus says "I am" again and again: "I am the light of the world." "I am the good shepherd." Jesus did call others to follow, but he was never coercive or invasive of the boundaries of others. He always gave people room to say no. And he never hesitated to challenge people to the point that they chose not to follow, as in the case of the rich young man. Jesus challenged him to sell his possessions. The man went away instead, and Jesus let him go. Inviting people to follow is very different from pursuing them.

❧ HOW TO LET GO OF OUTCOMES
Letting go is a profoundly spiritual action. It means we recognize our own limitations, and acknowledge that we are not ultimately in charge: God is. It is humbling, freeing, and empowering for ourselves and others. Like all spiritual tasks, it takes time. I do not have three easy steps to letting go,

because there's nothing easy about it. Yet here are three things to pay attention to as you think about how you might let go:

- Remember that controlling others is impossible.

- Focus on your own clarity. You cannot control how things turn out, but you can figure out what you think.

- Consider how you need to articulate your views to others. Disciplining yourself to say what you think in a self-defined manner can be a way to let go.

As with so many other vital spiritual tasks, we never let go once and for all. We are involved in a long-term endeavor that involves letting go again and again. When I notice my own willfulness and attempts to control others, I have to bring myself back to my own vision and beliefs. I have to think through how to define myself to others. Then I start the process all over again. When I can stick with it, I notice the difference in myself and in the way others respond to me.

TAKING THE LONG VIEW

As we manage ourselves in relation to the outcome we hope for, we need patience. Often we only look at one year, or perhaps five. But a longer perspective may be more realistic. Once at a seminary panel discussion a student asked, "Do you have any advice for us?" I answered with my usual catch-phrase, "Everything takes five years." The audience laughed. Afterward, my colleague, Israel Galindo, author of *The Hidden Lives of Congregations,* said to me, "I think you're too optimistic!" Galindo suggests that it takes five years for a clergy leader to get to the point of knowing a congregation well enough even to begin to articulate a vision for the congregation.[17]

"Culture change" is evolutionary, not revolutionary—and never underestimate the power of the old culture to stick around. Many denominations have transformational or church revitalization initiatives that are meant to turn struggling and declining congregations into vital churches engaged with their communities. Yet as valuable as these goals are, they are part of the anxious, quick-fix mentality that pervades our society. Congregations and denominations are declining, and everyone is worried about it. No one knows quite what to do. This trend extends beyond the mainline churches to evangelical denominations as well.[18] Anxious clergy, pressured by anxious denominational officials, can engage in these efforts to try to whip their congregations into shape. They use well-meaning methods in a willful way that does not benefit the leader-church relationship and that is unlikely to bear significant fruit in the long term. Quick fixes do not promote the health of the congregation; an anxious response to a problem rarely leads to a productive outcome.

No clergy leader can transform a congregation; no CEO can transform a company. Change happens organically, in the relationship between the leader and the led, and it takes time. We live in an impatient society that may not give change the time it needs. But we can set our own goals, and work with those we lead for the long term. We need to be fully engaged with the effort and recognize that the process will take a long time.

Patience is an essential part of letting go. The world may be changing faster than it did in the past, but human emotional process is the same. People still resist change, still take time to assimilate it, still take time to develop relationships. Leadership now, as then, requires infinite patience, persistence, and a willingness to look at the horizon, to imagine what cannot yet be seen.

The radical economist E. F. Schumacher long ago contrasted "convergent" and "divergent" problems. "Convergent" problems are technical problems that can be solved by reasoning, and the solution can be passed along to later generations. We are very good at solving those problems today.

"Divergent" problems are human problems that every generation struggles with. These problems simply have to be lived out. As Schumacher said, they "have no solution in the ordinary sense of the word."[19] Church leaders need to work on the "divergent" problems, the problems of how people live and work together. It is not easy, and it takes time, lots of it—both time out of our schedule and time on the calendar. A presbytery executive interviewed for the Pulpit and Pew study of clergy satisfaction remembers someone saying to him, "When you go to a new ministry, you should plant a peach tree, and do not expect your ministry to bear fruit before that peach tree does. Well, it takes three years before you get a peach off that tree."[20] For significant movement in a congregation, that may be just the beginning.

Yet patient leadership does not mean passive leadership. Leaders must take action, and lots of it, over a long period of time, for their work to have a lasting impact. There is always something interesting to do. We are less likely to fume with impatience and frustration when we recognize the reality that growth and change take a long time.

❧ QUESTIONS TO PONDER

It takes nerve for a leader to stay on course, and there is a very real risk that the voices of impatience will win out. This path is not for the faint of heart. But for those leaders who long to make a real difference in the world, even in a small way, and who are tired of spinning their wheels, this way offers more potential for growth, less unproductive stress, and a new framework for looking at the task of leadership in today's world.

Here are five questions to consider in thinking about your own leadership:

- Where have I been pushing too hard? How could I step back?

- Where do I need to clarify my own thinking?

- Where do I need to define myself more clearly?

- In what endeavors am I most inclined to be willful: worship? a favorite program? my family life?

- How long am I willing to work on this project (whatever it is)?

CHAPTER 7

UNDERSTAND
MONEY

Saint Matthew is traditionally the patron saint of bankers, accountants, and bookkeepers. Two paintings of Matthew illustrate different approaches to money in congregational life. One, by the Flemish artist Jan Sanders Van Hemessen, shows Matthew in his countinghouse, his eyes focused on his desk, which is covered with coins. Jesus stands off to the side, his face alight and his hand raised, trying to get Matthew's attention, but Matthew is so focused on the money he cannot pay attention to Jesus' call. This painting reminds me of a parish that receives an invitation to join in a community ministry to youth. They are facing a tight budget this year, and decide they cannot spare the funds necessary to partner in this ministry. This refusal is not the first time: every time this congregation is invited to expand its ministry, it declines because of a sense of financial scarcity. They, too, are so focused on the money they cannot hear the call.

In a second painting, by Giovanni Girolamo Savoldo, Matthew is receiving the gospel from an inspiring angel. His paper and pen are on the desk before him, but his head is lifted and turned toward the angel, ready to hear the message. He has moved beyond his obsession with money to an openness to God's call in new ways. This image is like a parish that decides to move forward with a new music ministry designed to bring neighbors into the church. They know it will cost them, but they believe the rewards will be worth it. As the leadership clearly shares their vision with the parish, they find church members coming forward with most of the needed funds. The leaders make the decision to move ahead, trusting that the rest of the money will come in.

When we have our head down like Matthew in the first painting, so focused on the money (in ministry, usually because we think there is not enough), we will find it hard to hear the call, the word about how we are to follow faithfully. But when we can lift up our heads and consider our calling first, clarifying our own principles and goals for ministry, we often will find that finances fall into place.

We might say that money makes the church go round, in more than one way. Congregations need financial resources to carry out their ministry, of course. But additionally, money makes the church go anxiously round in circles, as we try to figure out how to raise the funds we need and worry about whether or not we will be able to do it.

Money is a high-stress issue in most congregations. Who gives how much is often secret, even from the pastor. Preaching about money is not easy, and as pastors we can feel frustrated that more people do not get it. Congregations struggle to meet their budget, let alone increase their ministry. And when pastor and people are both anxious, it is hard to make real progress. People find their moods following the ups and downs of the stock market. They read an article on saving for retirement in the morning and head for the mall in the afternoon. We are constantly worried about money, but we do not know what to do about it.

Clergy themselves have a complicated relationship with money, especially in congregational life. They carry the anxiety for whether the budget is met and the ministry can go on. They worry about their own salaries and those of their staff. They watch the choices their church members make around money, and they wonder why. The result is that for most pastors, stewardship season is not a favorite time of year. "How can we get these people to support the ministry?" "How can we get them to understand the mission?" "Why don't more people tithe?" "Will we be able to support the budget?" "Will I get a raise this year?"

∾ IT'S NOT ABOUT THE MONEY

The reality of church finance is that when someone says, "It's about the money," it is not really about the money. Rather, money becomes a focus for and an expression of anxiety in the congregation. Money challenges are a symptom of deeper forces at work in congregational life, whether these forces arise from the long-term history of the congregation or a current spike in anxiety. These money issues highlight the processes at work in a congregation and allow them to become visible.

When we track how leaders and other church members function around finances, we can learn a lot about our community. Some people become overinvolved in congregational life through their giving, wanting to control how decisions are made. Others use money to distance, reducing their giving when they are dissatisfied. We can watch who is able to make clear decisions about money and who gets most anxious when the church experiences financial challenges, and then we can more clearly assess the health and vitality of our congregation.

Money is a focus for anxiety because money is fundamentally about survival. Individuals need money to live; churches need money to maintain themselves. It becomes cyclical: we are anxious so we focus on money; our money problems get worse as a result; we become more anxious. The cycle can perpetuate itself right into the death of a congregation, or at least the departure of a pastor. How can we begin to look at problems around money as symptoms and learn to assess the wider story, rather than focusing all our attention on the financial difficulties?

In my own ministry in the local church, I often dreaded stewardship time. I can remember thinking I could hardly wait for the stewardship campaign to be over so I could get back to "real" ministry. This meant I had some growing to do. As I learned more about my own family story, I discovered some of the multigenerational forces that were driving my anxiety about money, and about stewardship in particular. For example, my grandmother on my father's side was cheated out of an inheritance as a young woman, and she bitterly resented that loss until she died. Depression-era financial struggles intensified her feeling of deprivation. My father was raised by her, and he raised me—so I inherited the sense of scarcity that was part of our family story. My grandfather on the other side was a pastor who raised five children on a small salary, also through the Depression years.

As I got more curious about my family story, I began to ask my parents and other family members questions about the family and money. I heard stories I had never heard before, including the fact that my frugal maternal grandmother, the pastor's wife, once spent $60 on a blouse—in 1916! On the other side of the family, my father's brother never hesitated to spend what he had. I learned there were more choices around money in my family than I had realized. A feeling of scarcity was not the only approach to money that was available to me. I began little by little to realize the possibility of a greater sense of freedom and abundance both in my personal life and in my ministry.

For pastoral leaders, our family history with money has an impact on how we lead. Take some time to examine your own family story. Here are some tips to begin the process:

- Observe your relatives' behavior with money—with curiosity and without criticism.

- ✧ Notice who saves and who spends, who makes a lot and who makes a little: uncles, aunts, and cousins as well as parents and siblings.

- ✧ Pay attention to the stories people tell about money. (Remember, they may or may not be true, even if everyone believes them!)

- ✧ Notice any gender differences around dealing with money.

- ✧ Learn what you can about previous generations' attitudes toward money.

The implications of this work go beyond ourselves, into our congregations and also into our own families. I know I have passed along some of my own anxiety about money to my children, and my own old patterns pop up from time to time. Recently, when my daughter came home from college, within an hour I was giving her a hard time about money! This time, at least, I noticed what I was doing while I was doing it, which I consider progress. And she and I were able to have a good laugh about it.

In my ministry, I began over time to view money challenges as symptoms. As I have said, financial problems in church are rarely about money, but almost always reflect anxiety in the congregation. With this perspective, I automatically became less anxious myself, and could ride out the natural ups and downs. So when I was getting ready for a sabbatical, I asked myself how the anxiety about my leaving might show up in the church. My immediate answer was: money. That fall as we were planning for my upcoming summer sabbatical, pledges were down for the first time in many years. But I stayed calm, the other leaders stayed calm—and giving during my summer leave was stronger than previous summers, and the year as a whole was fine.

When congregational anxiety gets focused on finances, ask questions such as, "Why now?" and, "What else is going on in the congregation?" Keep your head and don't panic, and you will be better able to marshal your resources and the resources of others to handle the challenge.

☙ KNOW YOUR CHURCH'S MONEY STORY

Understanding the congregation's history with money, as well as our own story, is an important factor in staying calm and flexible around stewardship. The Reverend Paul Thomas, pastor of the Evangelical Congregational Church (United Church of Christ) in Westborough, Massachusetts, discovered this when the church celebrated its 275th anniversary. He learned about the first settled pastor, Ebenezer Parkman, who stayed for fifty-eight years, with an influential ministry in the church and community. Parkman struggled with his church leaders through those years to make sure his pay and his allotment of firewood was provided. He even had to ask for money on his deathbed. In Parkman's diary of 1781 he wrote, "I am going blind and it is sore times for me as my people have paid me no penny for fifteen months." Thomas realized that the current struggles around money in the congregation were part of a much longer story. As a result, he says, "I have tried to get light and playful about the financial stresses and strains, and remind them about Ebenezer Parkman's story and the systemic issues around money." His strategic use of the Parkman story helps defuse some of the anxious focus on money in this church's history.

Still, the past is always present, and it is worth our time to learn the congregation's story in this important area. Points to consider include:

- ☙ What was the attitude of the founders toward the support of the ministry?

- ☙ How was the building financed?

- ☙ What financial crises have been faced, and how were they handled?

๑ What are the year-to-year giving patterns over the
long term?

As you learn these facts, you will be better able to make sense
of current attitudes toward finances in the parish.

One church began its ministry, as most church starts do,
without enough resources. Yet in this case the leadership
stumbled along for years without marshalling enough to support the ministry. There never seemed to be enough. The
legacy of that rocky start is a persistent feeling, decades later,
that there is not enough and never will be. In this congregation there has also always been a good deal of secrecy around
money, and a willingness to let the leadership take responsibility for money matters. Fortunately, there has been a trend
toward greater openness in recent years, but patterns like this
in a church take a long time to shift. Clear leadership in
financial matters is always beneficial. Yet even as we work for
greater clarity and flexibility around money in the congregation, patience is essential.

Paul Thomas also says that he asks the church board, and
the church as a whole, "directly, regularly, and unflinchingly
to support the ministry of the church." When we can recognize those historical forces at work, calm down, and simply
challenge people to support the ministry of the church, people are better able to hear and respond. As in other areas of
leadership, we are giving room to follow, while making the
challenge clear.

Thomas says, "I try very hard not to take it all too personally." One of the difficulties when challenging people to
give can be that our own salary is part of the picture. But
even when our salary is at issue, the less we take it personally
the better. There are always larger forces at work in the congregation.

๑ ASSESSING YOUR CHURCH
Charles W. Collier, senior philanthropic adviser at Harvard
University, works with families to help them make effective

decisions surrounding their financial wealth and family philanthropy. "Money is often an object of anxiety in the family," he says, "whether it is scarcity or abundance." His observations of families that do better with money apply to churches as well. As we have seen, money is an object of anxiety in church life as well. In an interview Charles Collier told me what he found:

- Families that fare better are more open around their money. There is less secrecy. *Church corollary:* churches that fare better have less secrecy and more openness.

- Families that fare better prepare the next generation and see money as a tool to enhance the launching of their children. *Church corollary:* churches that fare better see their money as a tool for ministry.

- Families that fare better care for others beyond their family. *Church corollary:* churches that fare better are focused on mission beyond their walls, not simply on meeting their own needs.

Churches, like families, can view money as a weapon, as evil, as emotionally fraught, as dangerous, as scarce, as a possession. A more neutral, open view of money sees it as a resource, a tool, an opportunity, a gift. This neutrality makes it easier to make decisions that can benefit the future of the family and its members—and the church and its members.

Understanding more deeply what is going on in your congregation is a key element of leading more easily around money. But there is more to it than that. Thinking through your own principles and goals about money, for yourself individually and for the congregation, will benefit you and the whole church. What are your own foundational beliefs about money and stewardship? What are your specific goals for the financial life of this congregation? How can you clearly state those goals without coercion and without telling people what they ought to be doing?

The Reverend Nancy Cox, rector of St. Mark's Episcopal Chapel in Storrs, Connecticut, says, "This is not my parish to save, it's Jesus', and that work has already been done. Churches organize themselves in many different ways, with buildings, and without, with paid staff, and without." She keeps asking, "What is this parish's prayerful vision for itself, and what do they need to make that happen?"

This can be difficult when we feel we must raise our own salary. We feel like we are being evaluated in the process. Cox says about the salary question, "My stipend is the biggest item in the budget. If I let people, they will make it about Nancy Cox, so I don't. This is the rector's stipend, and this parish has decided to have a full-time rector. So, whoever is in this position, this is how the position has to be funded."

Offering the challenge to give more by stating our own convictions and painting a picture of our vision for the ministry of the church that can be possible with increased giving is very different from telling people they should give more. Pastoral leaders can step away from trying to convince others to think correctly and act correctly, and begin to state clearly their own position and beliefs about this critically important issue. When we do this, we can find our message clearer and our stress reduced. We can use our own self-definition to challenge others. We spend a lot of effort telling people how they ought to think and behave about money. Yet in this area of ministry, like all others, it is always more effective to say "I" ("I believe," "I choose") rather than "you" ("you ought," "you should," "you need to"). People resist being told what to do, and they are drawn toward leaders who are clearly self-defined.

❧ FACING A FINANCIAL CRISIS

What about those times of financial crunch, which happen in every church, when everyone's anxiety is high? Most parishes face financial challenges from time to time. The largest giver moves away. A church conflict leads to giving far below the budget. An economic downturn means people give less and church investments return less, leading to a double-barreled blow to expected income. A capital campaign falls well short of the goal.

As always, if we can be clear about our own principles and goals, our anxiety will be lower, and that will help everyone else. Calm, like panic, is contagious. Anxious leaders will find it harder to make good decisions about money, even at the best of times. In a crisis, the more we can manage our anxiety, the better the decisions we will make. If a key meeting is coming up, think through your own goals for the meeting. Possible goals include:

- "I want to keep my sense of humor through the meeting."

- "I want to clearly state what my bottom line is for my salary package next year, without getting defensive."

- "I want to talk less than I usually do," or conversely,

- "I want to make sure to state my point of view rather than letting others dominate."

We can also coach other congregational leaders to be clearer and calmer in the middle of a crisis. Larry Matthews describes a financial crisis that arose in the church he led shortly after he announced his retirement after thirty-two years. The pledge campaign came in surprisingly low. Matthews began by recognizing this was not a financial problem primarily, but a symptom of heightened anxiety due to his upcoming retirement. Before the meeting of the administrative committee to discuss this challenge, he consulted with the chair, and shared his understanding of the challenge at hand. "He just happened to have a great sense of humor, and he also had some understanding of systems thinking,"

Matthews says. He suggested to the chair that the chair's job at the beginning was to get the committee laughing, so that their anxiety could go down.

"I'm not sure how I'm going to do that, but I think I can do it," he said. The meeting was a success, and over the next several months the leadership stayed calm, and was able to guide the congregation through a second pledge campaign and a thoughtful budgeting process. Matthews also had goals for himself at every meeting, particularly to work on his own self-regulation, and to challenge the leadership to see the bigger picture and not simply work for a quick-fix solution.

One fact that came out was that one family was giving a huge percentage of the budget, and the congregation unknowingly had become dependent on their giving. So the crisis was an opportunity to challenge the rest of the congregation to be more responsible as well as more generous in their giving. This church had originally been founded as a mission congregation, with a heavy dependency on the sponsoring bodies at the beginning. This dependency was still present in the congregation, playing out in a heavy reliance on this one family to carry the budget. The patterns of past generations are always still present in one way or another, and it pays to keep our eyes open to look for them.

When anxiety is high, look for those who are calmer, and coach them to exercise their leadership. Watch for people who can define themselves, rather than tell people what they ought to do. Over time, try to get these people into official leadership roles in the congregation. This can make a big difference when the next crisis comes along.

Simply lightening up about money can help the congregation make better decisions, because when we feel under threat, it is hard to think straight. When I was a pastor, I collected cartoons about money to read before executive board meetings. Sometimes I shared them, sometimes I chose not to. But the effect was to make me less anxious which helped me function better in the meetings.

Here are some questions to consider as we assess where our responsibility as leaders lies:

- What am I responsible for, and what belongs to others?

- Am I trying to balance the church budget on my own back?

- Am I staying awake at night while everyone else sleeps like a baby?

- Am I the biggest single giver in the congregation?

∽ OVERFUNCTIONING WITH MONEY

Overfunctioning can show up in the area of finances just as in other areas of congregational life. In many congregations, a small percentage of the people give most of the money. Sometimes clergy turn down a raise to help balance the church budget. In some churches, one family steps in at the end of the year to make up the shortfall, year after year. Overfunctioning can show up not only in dollars but also in how information is shared: the way a few protect the rest of the congregation by keeping secrets about financial challenges.

Our task is to function, to be a responsible leader, without overfunctioning. The line is a subtle one. As Friedman often said, "It's not what you do, but how you do it." So it is not a matter of merely following specific rules or guidelines, but of managing our own anxiety, trying to think as clearly as we can, and acting thoughtfully as a result. That said, the tasks of leadership are:

1) to be honest about the current reality;

2) to paint a picture of the possible future; and

3) to challenge the congregation to do their part to make the future possible.

The art of these tasks is to carry them out while keeping our own anxiety down, and not to try to will people to see things from our point of view. If current reality is painful, and people do not want to see it, saying it louder will not do the trick. If the vision of the future is something they do not want to see, trying harder to convince them will not work. What's a leader to do? Larry Matthews likes to use this phrase: "That's just how I see it."

And it is always important to remember this: if you make shifts in your functioning around money in the congregation, chances are there will be some reaction. If you take a bold move forward, giving may go down, temporarily. In a congregational system everything is interconnected, so do not be surprised by the pushback. It is inevitable, and it may be a sign you are on the right track. We will deal better with the reactivity of others when we can hold a position of curiosity, noticing how people respond without wishing, "if only these people were different." Frustrated impatience rarely produces results, although these feelings may be inevitable from time to time. Instead, when we can accept people as they are, while continuing to offer a challenge to grow, they will find it easier to respond to our leadership in the important area of stewardship.

✒ QUESTIONS TO PONDER

Powerful forces are at work in our society and in our churches, as well as in ourselves. Yet we and those we lead do not need to be at the mercy of those forces. As we gain a clearer vision for the ministry of stewardship in our congregations, we can challenge ourselves and others to growth and greater freedom. Our relationship with money, like all high-anxiety issues, can be a lifetime of work, but as pastoral leaders we are called to make this journey and to call others to join us. We will remember that we are not to be anxious about our lives, for "is not life more than food, and the body more than clothing?" (Matthew 6:25). Then we will be hijacked less often by our own fears and the fears of others, because we can return again and again to the clarity of our own calling. And, over time, we will find that understanding the role of money, and leading our churches in this crucial area, becomes easier.

Here are ten questions to ask yourself about your church and money:

- How are decisions about money made?

- What do I know about the history of money in the congregation? What are the long-term patterns around money?

- How much are questions about money discussed openly in the congregation? Who knows who gives what? Who knows how much the pastor gives?

- Do people use their giving to distance themselves from the congregation or to try to control the leadership?

- How open is the congregation to receiving a challenge around giving?

- Do I notice a connection between money issues and other events in congregational life?

- How serious and emotionally intense are people about money?

- When I change my functioning around money, how do I notice people reacting? (For example, giving a more challenging stewardship sermon, asking for a raise for the first time, taking a financial crunch less seriously.)

- What do I know about my own family story as it relates to money?

CHAPTER 8

LEAD AND
DO NOT PANIC

Barbara is sitting in her office when the phone rings to alert her to one of parish ministry's worst nightmares: her youth director has been arrested for selling drugs. Her heart starts to pound and her body is overtaken by anxiety. As she hangs up the phone, her mind spins out the scenario: angry parents in her office, headlines in the local paper, disaster for the church. The parish is a suburban congregation that has always prided itself on its youth ministry. There is a lot of competition among churches in the community to offer the best youth program. The church increased the job to full time and hired the son of some key leaders in the congregation. Barbara was not sure about hiring a church member, but went along with it. Still, she has been delighted with his work and the way he has fit in with the staff and her own goals—until now.

In another congregation, a crisis builds gradually and then comes to a head over growing disapproval of the pastor's leadership style. Steve knew this was happening, but hoped it would settle down if he just ignored it. A small yet vocal contingent has rallied enough support, and the moderator has decided to call a special business meeting to discuss it. He will not listen to Steve's worries about the process. The meeting is Sunday, and Steve is afraid he will soon be out of a job.

A crisis is a critical moment in an organization's life that could well turn out to be a disaster. We usually perceive it as negative at the time—we wish it had not happened. At crisis time, anxiety goes up. Crises in church life range from a drastic budget shortfall to the discovery of sexual misconduct to a building-destroying fire. Smaller crises, such as sudden conflict over a staff member or a worship experience, can be almost as hard to handle.

All leadership crises have some common denominators. First, something is at risk: a ministry, a relationship, church finances, even our job. Second, anxiety—ours and others'—suddenly rises, making it more difficult to be thoughtful. Third, people typically look to us to do something about the crisis, which can cause our anxiety to spike even more.

Crises come to us in a variety of ways. Our own leadership efforts can sometimes precipitate a crisis. We are leading the congregation forward in new ways, and the inevitable reactivity and resistance reaches a peak that must be addressed. We finally make the decision to let a beloved staff member go and a firestorm erupts. Or we have a personal crisis that affects our ministry, such as a difficult divorce.

Sometimes the crisis chooses us. A fire destroys the church building. A major employer in the community shuts down. A natural disaster, small or large, hits the area. Hurricane Katrina affected churches all along the Gulf Coast, both directly by destroying church buildings and indirectly by damaging the economy and scattering the area's population.

However the crisis came to be, it is hard to see our way forward when we are in the middle of it. We lie awake at night considering options. People come to us with their anxieties, making it even harder to think clearly. We may work longer hours, and the physical and emotional effort may wear us out, so it is essential to remember that in any crisis, our own response contributes to the outcome. We are not simply at the mercy of events. When the unexpected hits, we will do much better if we keep our heads and respond thoughtfully, not simply react. Our response can keep a minor crisis from turning into a major one.

When a crisis comes, our very identity can be called into question. Who am I if I let things get to this point? If I were a good leader, we wouldn't be in this spot: we would have more people, and we would have more money. If I had taken more of a stand with these difficult board members, the conflict wouldn't have spiraled out of control. That is another reason why crises are so difficult: they involve not just the immediate problem, but also what that problem says to us and what we think it says to others about us. We feel exposed and vulnerable.

In times of crisis it is easy to blame others: If they weren't so recalcitrant, irresponsible, or difficult, we wouldn't be in this crisis. If the board had been willing to make a decision about that staff member, we wouldn't be in this mess. If people just gave enough money, we wouldn't have this budget emergency.

Here are six tips for handling any crisis, whatever its source. Crises vary and our strategy of response may vary as well, but the most important element in a crisis—how we manage ourselves—does not. Tips one and two will help you respond better in the moment the crisis breaks; the remainder will help you as you continue to respond, remembering that some crises take time to resolve.

1) Focus on yourself first.
Your own functioning is critical: you need to handle yourself, not the crisis. If you can keep your own anxiety down, everyone will make better decisions.

2) Breathe.
Oxygen literally helps your brain work better. When you feel your heart start pounding, stop and take a few deep breaths.

Whenever your anxiety begins to rise, stay focused on your own functioning, and keep breathing.

3) Think.
If you can reflect on the crisis rather than simply reacting to it, you will be better able to manage yourself.

4) Assess your resources: internal and external.
Look within for needed spiritual resources, and look around you for other key leaders who can keep their heads.

5) Get thoughtful counsel.
We often go looking for advice in a crisis, but choose your advisers carefully; look for those who can ask good questions, and offer a challenge along with the necessary hand-holding. Spend time with people who are calmer than you are.

6) Pray, meditate, or do whatever works to help you get the bigger picture.
Remember Luke's parable of the house built on rock: "That one is like a man building a house, who dug deeply and laid the foundation on rock; when a flood arose, the river burst against that house but could not shake it, because it had been well built" (Luke 6:48).

Most crises are not as disastrous as the initial panic indicates. It is possible the worst may happen; if so, keep your attention on yourself and your own functioning, rather than the response of others. But if you can keep your head and thoughtfully take steps to respond, often the turmoil will subside, and you can keep moving toward your goals.

When a crisis breaks, we can begin to cope with it by remembering the roots of our faith: Jesus' disciples faced a huge crisis in the crucifixion. At first the gospels show the disciples as terrified by the danger, but after the resurrection they are seen embracing the opportunity. A crisis means both danger and opportunity, and in the case of the cross, this was true. Out of the danger and opportunity of the cross, the earliest Christians created something new: the church. After a difficult and fearful beginning, they responded differently, and embraced the challenge offered. So can we.

⬲ SURVIVING A CRISIS

Antarctic explorer Ernest Shackleton's story shows that making it through a crisis is possible even when survival seems unlikely. After a disaster that could have meant death for his entire expedition, he brought everyone back alive. While his environment was strikingly different, his approach to leadership can help us survive a church crisis today. Like him, we are engaged in an effort that can seem impossible. We are trying to lead in a very challenging, even hostile environment. Shackleton paid attention to things we need to pay attention to, including his goal and his people, and he simply persisted when survival seemed unlikely. We can learn from him how our response in leadership can make a difference in a crisis.

Shackleton embarked on an expedition to cross the continent of Antarctica in 1914, his third such attempt. The *Endurance* (after the Shackleton family motto, "By endurance we conquer") set sail in August, and on November 5 the ship arrived at a whaling station on South Georgia Island in the South Atlantic, about one thousand miles from the Antarctic Peninsula. This would be their last contact with land for nearly two years. By January 15, 1915, they were within two hundred miles of their goal. But by January 24 they were beset, stuck in the ice.[21]

Shackleton knew the expedition would likely never proceed. He quickly shifted his vision from crossing Antarctica to the more immediate need for survival. The ship's surgeon, Alexander Macklin, wrote in his diary, "Shackleton at this time showed one of his sparks of real greatness. He did not rage at all, or show outwardly the slightest sign of disappointment; he told us simply and calmly that we must winter in the Pack, explained its dangers and possibilities; never lost his optimism, and prepared for Winter."[22]

The expedition crew waited through the long winter months. But when the breakup of the ice began at last, it foretold disaster. The pressure of the pack ice began to crush the *Endurance,* and finally on October 24, 1915, they had to abandon ship. They watched the ship that had brought them from England sink beneath the ice, leaving them thousands of miles from home with no way to get help. Once the ship sank, Shackleton once again had to develop a new vision quickly, if the group was to survive. He imagined it, and his vision became reality.

To survive a crisis, today's leaders must also be flexible, open to feedback from their environment. They have to recognize when circumstances are beyond their control, and when they need to adapt their goals to reflect reality. One aspect of letting go of the outcome is the ability to shift the vision when necessary. Leaders need discernment to know when to push through and when to make a change.

Moments of crisis test our leadership in ways that are also the keys to handling them. First, a crisis tests our *clarity:* how we figure out what we think in a time of high anxiety. Second, it tests our *connections:* how we manage relationships through the crisis. Third, it tests our *creativity:* how we discern ways to handle the crisis. And finally, it tests our *courage:* how we keep going through the pressures of a crisis.

ᔆ CLARITY

If we are going to handle the crisis effectively, we need to become clearer in our own thinking by stepping out of the emotional currents swirling around the situation. Assessing the crisis itself is an important part of getting clarity. It is important to ask the question, "Why now?" Why is this issue arising now? For example, a crisis can emerge in response to a leadership move on our part. In Barbara's case, the board had begun to move forward with a major worship initiative, and the crisis with the youth director seemed unrelated to the new direction. Yet church systems resist change in many ways. All parts of congregational life are connected, like a mobile. Disturb one part (in this case worship) and another (the youth group) may begin to vibrate.

Barbara and the other church leaders must respond to the youth minister's arrest. She may have to slow down her efforts to develop the new worship program. Still, it is better in most cases if she and the rest of the leaders can keep moving in general toward the goals they have articulated, staying on track with their purpose. Starting with our own clarity is critical. If we consider our own perspective as calmly as possible, that calm communicates itself to others. Anxiety is contagious, but so are thoughtfulness and calm.

We need to take time to reflect and discern what God is calling us to do. If we are well-grounded spiritually, we will be better able to think clearly when we are flooded with anxiety. It is easy to poll others on what they think, but it is more important to figure out what *we* think. This does not mean we ignore or dismiss the perspectives of others, but it does mean recognizing the fact that in a crisis we do not necessarily get what we want. A ministry may come to an end. The church may not meet the budget. We may not even get to keep our job. In the case of Pastor Steve, he may or may not be able to control whether there is a business meeting to discuss his ministry. But he can make choices about how he manages himself before the meeting, what he says at the meeting, and how he relates both to his supporters and detractors. While we do not cause a good outcome by what we do and we cannot guarantee anything, to ourselves or to others, our self-management is one important input to a system in crisis. And our response can call forth a different response from others, adding more constructive and creative input to the crisis management.

❧ CONNECTION

A leader affects the whole, whether it is a small band of explorers or a large denomination. The leader's influence does not come primarily from expertise or effort, but from the nature of his or her presence. Shackleton stayed closely connected to his men, constantly aware of what was going on with his group. He carefully balanced the needs of all, making sure that the sailors especially had what they required, not simply the higher ranks. He took care of those who needed it, but not too much. He even made sure that even when they were abandoning ship they had a banjo for song to keep morale up. Shackleton paid meticulous attention to everything, including tent assignments when they were camped on the ice.

You cannot survive a leadership crisis alone. It is essential to have allies, and to keep relating to them through the crisis. For church leaders in a crisis, you need to pay attention to those around you who can help the congregation make it through. Look around and assess your allies, paying particular attention to emotional maturity.

What if you are not the top leader in a crisis? You still have the important work of managing yourself. You cannot control the choices the leader makes, but you can think through your own position, the stands you need to take, and how to stay connected with that leader. If you are calm, others will likely gravitate to you. In this situation, watch for triangles, and be sure to stay in your role.

Shackleton constantly challenged the men to keep going. Because he did not ask them to do anything he was not willing to do himself, they were willing to do more than they thought they could. It can be tempting for us to protect people from the reality of a crisis, but it is more important for leaders to offer a challenge. You may be surprised by the response. In a time of acute anxiety, people often rise to the occasion. You can ask questions like: Who needs to know what is going on? How should we inform them? How can we ask them to contribute? This can be an opportunity to challenge people to step up and grow up. Through preaching, teaching, meetings, and conversations, we can issue the challenge to greater maturity and to the wider vision. We and others may one day look back on a crisis as a great gift.

When Shackleton and his men set out across the ice, after several days of grueling travel, one of the men announced he would go no farther. This was a dangerous time for the expedition: until now, everyone had followed Shackleton unquestioningly. He had to take a stand, yet he also recognized they could not maintain that pace, so they camped out and waited for the moving ice to bring them to open water. By this mix of firmness and flexibility Shackleton displayed what Friedman often described as the "keys to the kingdom," the ability to deal with sabotage.

Church leaders can find it hard to find the nerve to stand up to the most difficult and immature people in the congregation. But without that ability, we will find them running the show, and they can spell trouble for the institution. When we can strengthen our own backbone and take a stand, everyone will benefit.[23]

✎ CREATIVITY

A crisis can be a gift to you: an opportunity to develop yourself under intense circumstances or to do something you have never done before. Perhaps you have always wanted to be a bolder, more directive leader. This moment may be your chance to try it out. Or perhaps you have felt stuck in your current ministry. Whether you survive this crisis or lose your position, things will be different from now on. Or perhaps you have wondered which leaders in the congregation really have what it takes to move forward in new ways: this moment may give you the chance to see unexpected gifts in them.

From Elephant Island, a piece of rock in the South Atlantic, Shackleton set out with a small crew in the largest of the lifeboats. Sixteen days later, after surviving a hurricane,

they landed on South Georgia Island. Yet there was more to
come. As daylight began to wane, they faced a long, declining snow slope to reach the whaling station. Shackleton suggested they slide down the slope, and they tied themselves
together. One of the men remembered, "We seemed to shoot
into space. For a moment my hair fairly stood on end. Then
quite suddenly I felt a glow, and knew that I was grinning! I
was actually enjoying it. . . . I yelled with excitement, and
found that Shackleton and Crean were yelling, too."[24]

Even at a challenging time, when we are not sure what is
happening next, we can find moments of fun, like the men
sliding down the snow slope. These can be unexpected, or
we can begin to look for them. We will actually make better
decisions if we can keep our sense of humor. Or an afternoon off to do something completely different may help us
come back with renewed stamina. We will not find our best
response if we are simply grinding out our work, day after
day, or spending every moment frantically searching for the
right solution. Crisis management requires creativity, both
initially and along the way. Shackleton had continually to
adjust what he was doing as the circumstances changed; we
also need to adjust our direction and adapt our strategy as we
navigate our way through a crisis.

Can we use our imagination even in a crisis, to experiment creatively with new possibilities? It is not easy, but if
we cultivate our clarity and stamina, we will be better able to
try something new. What worked yesterday may not work
tomorrow, no matter how brilliantly it was conceived. We
need to keep thinking, imagining, and experimenting. In the
case of the youth group leader who was arrested, this could
mean turning the crisis into an opportunity for Barbara to
lead the parish in rethinking the youth program—its purpose, direction, and staffing. A new kind of youth ministry
might emerge. Without the crisis, they might have gone on
for years with the same model, even though it had never
reached as many kids and families as they hoped. A crisis

demands energy and creativity, but it can also release us for new possibilities.

∾ COURAGE

Leaders need courage: they need the ability to persist despite fear, discouragement, and setbacks. Shackleton showed an amazing ability to keep going or to try something new, to adjust his plans to deal with reality, but never lose sight of the goal, survival. His stamina was unbelievable. His men faced extraordinarily difficult conditions, but his situation was the most difficult of all. He was the leader, and so he was alone in the responsibility he carried. And yet he retained his optimism. One of his most pessimistic men wrote in his journal when they were stuck in the ship: "He is always able to keep his troubles under and show a bold front. His unfailing cheeriness means a lot to a band of disappointed explorers like ourselves. . . . He is one of the greatest optimists living."[25]

If you are the top leader in a crisis, you cannot escape the loneliness of leadership. You have to "keep your troubles under," to a point. No one else bears the responsibility you do. Other people are essential and can help support you, but Harry Truman was right about the buck stopping at the president's desk. In a church, the buck stops at the minister's desk. The burden can seem heavy, and sometimes we can feel we are not up to the challenge.

There is an important relationship between a hostile environment and the way we respond to it. In an environment that is too hostile, ultimately the response of the organism does not matter: if your plane crashes in flames, you are likely doomed no matter how you respond. Shackleton faced a strikingly difficult environment, and his response was an essential factor to the outcome. He had stamina and resolve. He was always well-connected to his men and very aware of his environment. He rarely became reactive even in the face of sabotage, and he could always see the bigger picture. He could imagine survival even when it seemed most unlikely.

In a crisis, this sort of courage is essential. Often the only way out is through, and things may get worse before they get better. As we move forward through the crisis, we may feel at times that everything is spiraling out of control. People are looking to us, and we do not know what to do. We hear criticism and complaints that intensify as the crisis continues. As a child, I had a child-size plastic toy clown called Bozo. He was weighted in the bottom, so if you punched him, he would bounce back up. No matter how many times you hit the clown, he would come back. He never took it personally. How do we develop that kind of stamina? Can we bounce back from criticism? Courageous leadership does require developing more neutrality. We do not have to become a punching bag, but we can remember that we need not take personally much of what comes our way.

We simply have to tough it out sometimes, and remember that things will settle down if we can keep our heads. Courage does not mean we are not anxious or afraid, but that we can act in spite of our fear. Instead of being surprised by crisis, we can simply be prepared for the fact that we have a hard job, and crises are going to arise. Shackleton's expedition came to an end, but our adventure in ministry is ongoing. We get through one crisis, and breathe a sigh of relief—and the phone rings again. Being a congregational leader, whether as senior leader, staff, or lay leadership, is rarely easy.

A strong spiritual life provides the kind of grounding that can enable us to sustain ourselves through crises and setbacks—even the most difficult ones. This enables us to see the bigger picture rather than focusing on the narrow issue in front of us. I come back again and again to the prayer of Teresa of Avila: "Let nothing disturb you, nothing frighten you; all things are passing, God never changes. Patient endurance attains to all things; who God possesses in nothing is wanting; alone God suffices." There have been times in my ministry when I have said this prayer every day, just as she did. We all need ways to sustain ourselves spiritually day by day, and this is never more true than in a crisis.

❧ Questions to Ponder

Shackleton never reached his goal of crossing the Antarctic continent, but he accomplished something at least as remarkable. After two years, the adventure ended without a life lost. Shackleton's vision, stamina, and creativity were essential to the survival of the expedition party. The challenges we face are physically not as difficult as Shackleton's adventure, nor is our physical survival at stake. But on another level, they are even more intimidating, because these challenges are constant and ongoing as we lead congregations into the future. For Shackleton, the moment of crisis was an opportunity. Despite the life and death struggle, he got that chance he had dreamed of: a great open boat journey.

This very crisis you are in right now can be a real opportunity. Here are ten questions to consider:

- Is there anything to be grateful for in the middle of this crisis?

- And how do I sense God's presence, even now?

- Why now? (Crises usually do not come out of nowhere.)

- Who else needs to share this responsibility?

- What is the worst that could happen, and how would I handle that?

- What crises has the church faced in the past? How did it come through?

- Who are the most thoughtful people in leadership in the congregation? How can I connect with them?

- What are five options for facing this crisis?

✍ What family members might support me in this crisis? How can I be in touch with them?

✍ What are my goals for myself in this crisis? (For example: I would like to state my own views calmly. I will continue to take my day off. I want to learn to connect in a neutral way with people who are criticizing me. I will get my profile ready so I can look for another position.)

CHAPTER 9

STAY
CONNECTED

I first started leading a congregation when I was twenty-six years old and was called to be the interim pastor of a primarily Spanish-speaking congregation. It was a small church, with about fifty people in worship each Sunday. One influential family dominated the church. We had some bumpy times along the way, and my initial three-month contract was almost not renewed as I worked on learning Spanish and they tried to get used to a woman pastor as their leader. Still, they kept me on, and I found my way through the next year, preaching bilingually, conducting my first funeral and my first baptism. When I was not struggling to write Spanish sermons, I spent most of my time visiting people in their homes and having meals with church members. One Sunday, when a woman missionary came to preach, she automatically went to the lectern. The moderator got up and escorted her to the pulpit. She stepped into the pulpit and said, "Things have changed in this church!" Before me, they had never had a woman in the pulpit.

Ten years later, I saw a woman from the central family in the congregation at a denominational convention. She came running over to me, calling, *"Mi pastora."* Despite my inexperience and my language struggles, I was able to occupy the role of pastor sufficiently that she still saw me that way years later. I can't say I knew enough to have a deliberate strategy, but the relationships I developed carried me through, and lasted over the years.

Leadership never happens in a vacuum, but among specific individuals in a particular context, which means we need to relate to them. Building these relationships is like building capital we can draw on when we want to challenge people to move forward in some new ways. If we do not take the time to make these connections, any changes we institute will be short-lived and will certainly not last beyond our tenure. The force for human togetherness is a powerful one, and leaders ignore it at their peril. In any church, large or small, we must be well-connected to key players, and find ways to communicate with everyone. Preachers, of course, have the pulpit, but it takes more than preaching to forge a solid connection with a congregation.

At the same time, leaders are not just one of the gang, and we have to be prepared to step apart from the group. Leaders have to be able to deal with the loneliness that ensues; we all want to be accepted, and it is hard to move apart. As I mentioned earlier, Ronald Heifetz describes this as the "view from the balcony," getting above the fray enough to have a wider perspective. Heifetz suggests viewing ourselves as a part of the dance even when we are viewing from the balcony. Finding the balance between connecting with people and stepping ahead of them to lead is the ongoing dance of community life.

So in addition to a clear sense of ourselves and our purpose, we need to pay attention to our relationships. The content of our ideas and the course we chart are critically important. Still, those relationships determine the outcome of our leadership endeavors as much as our direction. The best leaders balance individuality and togetherness, moving ahead while fostering close ties with their followers. This is called "differentiated leadership" and at its most basic, it involves maintaining ourselves and staying in relationship with those around us.

Leaders need to find the right balance between closeness and distance. You cannot minister or lead in isolation. Still, solitude is necessary: you do need the time alone to think and pray. Yet then you need to come back into the fray, to connect with all the people: the ones you love as well as the ones who drive you up a wall.

✍ FINDING A BALANCE

It is not easy to find this balance in relationship. We have all known leaders who were too close to their followers. The need to be liked drives many of their decisions, or they simply are unaware of the need for boundaries. They lose perspective on their position. Ultimately, they become ineffective because they are unable to take a stand. Clergy sexual misconduct may be the most extreme example of getting too close in congregational life. But a pastoral leader who simply avoids conflict by never taking a stand may also be too close. And a priest whose entire social life revolves around the congregation may have trouble finding enough distance to lead.

We have also known leaders who were too distant. A rector under stress may spend more and more time in his office, doing administrative work and preparing sermons. He attends meetings but leaves as soon as they are done. He avoids those who are criticizing him even as his anxiety increases, but by doing so he jeopardizes his ministry. He plays his part in the choices that ultimately lead to a crisis. Another priest may use denominational involvement as a way to distance herself from a parish she feels unsuited for. Or a minister distracted by family worries may not have the energy to connect appropriately. In all these cases, being too distant from the parish makes leadership difficult, because the substantive relationships to support it are not there.

Finding the balance between too close and not close enough takes energy and attention. We face two related challenges: first, to lead without taking on the anxiety of our followers (allowing them to get in our space). This does not mean we never listen to the worries of our people. It does mean we work to be clear on which worries belong to us and which do not. Others will be glad to hand us their anxiety, which can keep us from responding thoughtfully. For example, if a parishioner is upset about a change in worship, he or she may want us to do something immediately. But if the change is part of a long-term strategy, worked on with the vestry, our task simply may be to keep talking with that member, to keep the relationship going while we continue to move forward with the strategy.

Second, as we have discussed, we need to lead without trying to will people to be different (getting in *their* space). This does not mean we do not have opinions or a point of view on the direction the congregation should move. But it does mean we acknowledge and respect differing points of view, giving people room to have their own opinion. Even when we must make a decision from the top, those decisions will work out better when we put in the time on relationship-building and when we do not willfully try to convince them of our perspective.

Integrity in leadership means not simply doing the right thing, but more fundamentally having boundaries: knowing where we end and other people begin. As we work on our relationships, we relate to others with respect and expect the same respect in return.

❧ HOW TO MAKE CONNECTIONS

Developing relationships in congregational life means we see this connection as part of our job. We intentionally devote time to it, and think strategically about how to make connections happen. There are as many ways to do it as there are leaders, but all leaders must do it.

I once met a business leader who understood the need for connection intuitively. Angelo Carella, when he was president of the Federal Reserve Bank of Portland, Oregon, spent half an hour a day walking around the floor, talking to as many people as he could. Every day. His tenure coincided with massive changes in the Federal Reserve Bank system. Employees were no longer essentially guaranteed a job for life, and many were worried about the changes. But despite the upheaval, his effort to stay connected with employees made a turbulent time easier. People continued to do their work effectively, and years after he retired, people still remembered the connection he had made with them.

Every leader needs to find his or her own way of connecting. This is not simply a management or leadership technique: Carella's behavior developed authentically out of who he was, and he knew his environment. The best leaders find out how to relate to others in a way that fits them, and in a way that fits their context. A church setting calls for a different kind of connection than a business. For a pastor who loves it, pastoral visitation can be a wonderful way to connect, even in today's fast-paced world. For another leader, a regular routine of phone calls to the vestry to check in at least monthly might serve the same purpose.

Another example of this type of connection is offered by the Reverend Robert "Odie" Odierna, an Episcopal priest in Nashua, New Hampshire. During his twenty-two years in his current parish, Odierna has spent one Sunday a month giving a question-and-answer sermon. Parishioners write down their questions on cards, and he gives his responses to the questions from the pulpit. He says, "It's given me a neat bird's-eye view: It teaches the preacher. It also gives people the chance to hear what I really think." He adds, "Knowing I'm honest, people can say what they want. There is no topic that is taboo: we've talked about sex, living together, homosexuality, abortion, dying." He views this practice as one of the foundation blocks of his relationship with the parish.

Once again, this is not a matter of adopting a technique, such as "management by walking around" or "question-and-

117

answer sermon." Sure, we can try out different ways to connect, but if we try to use techniques, people sense phoniness
and resent it. We may strategize for ways to develop relationships, but finally, we have to be as fully present as we can be
with the people we lead. We have to show up, breathe, look
them in the eye, and say what we really believe. Leadership is
about *how* we say it, as well as *what* we say. When we are truly
present with people, they know it. When we are on autopi-
lot, they know it. Over time a dynamic relationship develops,
and trust increases. We learn their cues, and they learn ours.
As leaders, we are part of an ensemble cast, and the give and
take contributes to the whole. They cannot do it without us,
and we cannot do it without them.

At times of uncertainty in my congregation, I would make
a list of key leaders in the congregation to call periodically,
particularly when church life got bumpy. We did not have to
talk about the issue at hand—in fact, I found this approach
often more effective when we discussed things that had nothing to do with church. The purpose of this effort was to make
sure I was maintaining a strong relationship with the leadership and through them with the congregation.

How do you decide which people you need to connect
with? Begin with the formal leaders: senior warden, president, or moderator; board or vestry members; committee
chairs; team leaders. Then consider the informal leaders: the
matriarch and/or patriarch; the founding members; and other
influential people. Every church has these leaders, and part
of your job is to know who they are and develop a plan for
connecting with them. It will solidify your relationship with
the congregation. Include both people who agree with you
and people who disagree with you. The point of the connection is not to convince them to agree with you, but to
build some emotional capital in the relationship. More solid
relationships will help you lead more effectively over time.

You know your people—or if you don't, find out about
them! Football, opera, their kids, their last trip: the topic does

not matter. This approach means we work on *connecting*, paying attention to the process as much as the content of the conversation. When we are well connected, people know it. We do not have to make an announcement, or tell people we are working on it. The presence of leadership is such that it makes itself known.

A leader does not need to make a personal connection with every individual to be engaged with everyone. In larger organizations this is impossible. But the leader's presence still matters, no matter how large the system. This is true even of a nation: as soon as George W. Bush returned to Washington on September 11, 2001, and particularly after he addressed the nation, every American was affected whether they knew it or not. This was not about politics, but about the connection between leader and led. When Bush took four days to get to New Orleans after Hurricane Katrina first hit, his lack of presence likewise affected every American, and particularly those in the hurricane-affected area.

In a large church, the senior leader has to think constantly about how he or she is maintaining a presence with the entire congregation. This is equally true of a bishop or executive in a denomination. Maintaining a presence is far more than a communication strategy: it is a way of thinking about the nature of leadership that can affect everything a leader does. Think through how you are maintaining your connection with those with whom you may not have a one-to-one relationship. Consider where you need to show up in person, by e-mail, or by phone in order to make this happen.

When leaders are thinking about relationships, they will act in different ways and make different decisions. For example, a rector could decide to attend the choir Christmas party even though it makes December even busier. He would know the impending retirement of the long-term director has raised anxiety, and believe his presence will make a connection that will benefit the system. Another pastor might prioritize her phone messages and e-mail not according to the content of the message—or the emotional tone—but based on the way she wants to connect with the congregation. She would give herself time to think before responding automatically to anxious messages.

⌘ TAKING A STAND WHILE TENDING RELATIONSHIPS

Staying connected to others in a mature way means being ourselves in relationship to them. We work to do this without being pulled into a comfortable harmony where we all have to agree. When we have to agree, there is not much opportunity for progress. This is a temptation for church leaders, because often we were socialized to be nice. A lack of conflict is viewed as a good thing, by both clergy and congregations. But it can get in the way of growth.

To pull apart from the crowd and take a clear stand can mean that we upset people, but when we put in the time building relationships it is easier to move through these difficult times. Leadership in a congregation takes time; building these relationships takes years. So when you walk in the door, the first thing is not vision, but relationships. The challenge over time is to take a stand and watch the reactivity heat up, manage yourself, and tend the relationships.

We need to distinguish between relationship process and short-term problems in the relationship: the reaction to Sunday's sermon, the budget shortfall, the disorganized youth director. Such problems demand our attention and often we do need to respond quickly to the anxious e-mail regarding last week's sermon, to the budget problem, or the matter of staff incompetence. But looking only at the content of the problem is not enough.

Paying attention to process means we are watching the overall pattern of relationships in the congregation, including our part in the pattern. We notice what happens when we or other leaders take a clear stand, no matter what the issue: who jumps on board immediately, who can be counted on to automatically disagree. We learn enough about the history of the congregation to assess how the relationship patterns in the present reflect the past. Perhaps people in this parish have always been critical of the rector's preaching. Maybe the person holding the job of youth director never does very well, no matter who it is, and perhaps we have contributed to this.

It can be a challenge to manage ourselves and relate to others when anxiety is high. When people are angry, fearful, or critical, we may be inclined to withdraw, to hide, or to go on vacation. But when we can stay in touch, the potential for a good outcome increases. More than any specific events, the leader's response to those events helps determine outcome. Leaders who keep their heads and do not panic can often keep small conflicts from spiraling into big ones.

Odie Odierna also talked to me about the use of humor in moving through the kind of small changes that can cause big upsets in a congregation. "We took down the hymnboard. If you want to get your people mad, take down the hymnboard! This was a top-down decision—we felt worship would be better without it." Instead, he wanted an electronic board that would let people in the congregation know where they were in the liturgy, so the service would be more accessible to visitors. "Everybody had a fit because they thought I was putting an electronic board in a Gothic building! But we put this electronic board in a gorgeous wood frame."

Then he announced to the congregation, "Okay, I'm so excited because we're beginning construction on the liturgy board, and I'm excited because I know next week you're going to hate it." His lighthearted approach defused the upset in the congregation. In another church, the conflict could have spiraled out of control. He still teases them: "If your pledges get to 100 percent [of the budget], you can have the hymnboard back." Of course, what also carried him through was his approach to building relationships over two decades, along with his ability not to react too much to those who were the most concerned about the change.

121

We have to take a stand at times on matters of greater importance than hymnboards, of course. Relationships in congregational life are often tested over matters of more substantive changes in worship. To upset the balance in your congregation, change the style of your worship, or start a second worship service. Either one will do! People relate to their worship experience on the very deepest level, and some have a visceral reaction to change. Worship can become an automatic focus for anxiety in the congregation. But if you lay the groundwork by establishing relationships ahead of time, over a number of years, you and the congregation will be better able to weather the storm. And the same principles apply as in the hymnboard story: if you can keep your sense of humor, and manage yourself well enough not to get too reactive, it is easier to move ahead and keep the relationships.

In fact, relationships get tested in every aspect of congregational life: worship, music, youth program, staff relationships, letting staff go, denominational conflict about sexuality, cutting the budget, increasing the budget. We can easily get focused on the content of any of these issues, and seek to argue rationally with people until they agree with our position. Or we can avoid conflict as much as possible and hide our own views. Neither of these approaches will be productive.

Instead, the tasks are these: first, we put all our energy into clarifying and articulating what we ourselves think on the one hand (without trying to convert anyone to our point of view); and second, we keep building relationships. This is the path of self-differentiated leadership. When we follow this path, people will intuitively know we are respecting them, and they will be better able to hear what we are saying.

Episcopal priest Ed Bacon emphasizes, "It's really important to call, write, take out for coffee or a meal people who are resistant." He suggests this is a way for the leader to show he or she is not identifying the person's "resistance" with who they are as a person and parishioner. And, while the leader needs to stay on track with his or her goals, adjusting direction in response to feedback is also essential. Staying on course "doesn't mean that you don't listen, and allow their points of view to affect your mid-course corrections." Then, he says, they recognize you value them.

Bacon believes the goal of the church's ministry is to "encourage and stir up self in others." The point of working on relationships is not to get our own way or to ensure everything goes smoothly, but to allow people to develop greater degrees of "self," so they grow up emotionally and spiritually. Congregations made up of mature people can weather the inevitable ups and downs rather than splitting apart or dwindling away. Instead, people are committed to their own growth, to each other, and to the health of the congregation and its work.

❧ OURSELVES IN RELATIONSHIP

To "stir up self" in others means we need an adequate sense of self ourselves. We need to know how to manage the balance between closeness and distance from others. We all grow up in families that to some degree do not know how to do this right. In our family we learn about relationships, and develop our instinctive responses to others. Some families are very good at closeness but do not know how to be separate. Some families are very good at distance but do not know how to be close. Understanding our own process and what it is we do in relationships will help us relate to others. (See chapter four for more on this essential topic.) Become a better observer of yourself, and you will be able to connect with others in a calmer and more effective way.

Pastoral counselor Meg Hess describes her own efforts to work on dealing with criticism. She says, "My inability to deal effectively with criticism can create distance in my relationships, rob me of valuable feedback and cause unnecessary wear and tear on my brain." She describes her own experience after someone criticized her sermon at the door. She worked hard to manage herself, and asked the critic at coffee hour what he did not like about the sermon. He gave her some useful feedback that she used to make the sermon better at the next service. She concludes, "Learning how to tolerate the displeasure of others involves facing our own anxiety and managing it more effectively."[26]

There is real potential for pain in relationships in congregational life. We actually have to increase our tolerance for our own pain in order to grow. We need to tolerate people being angry or disapproving of us, and to deal with our discomfort at relating to them. Working on relationships is as much about us as it is about the other people. I play a part in all my difficult relationships: I want to blame the other, but it always takes two for there to be a problem, and I need to be honest enough to look at how I play my part. Fortunately or unfortunately, it always comes back to me, since that is what I can control.

So learn to know what is going on with yourself. Time to reflect is essential, along with some outside help to discern your own patterns of behavior. When you become anxious, do you withdraw or become more aggressive? Do you go numb? Do you shut down or start talking too much? The more you observe what it is you do, the better you can relate to people in congregational life, both those you find it easy to relate to and those who seem more difficult. You cannot make a different choice if you do not know what you do. Whatever your leadership position, knowing and managing yourself will benefit you more than anything else you can do.

⤳ LEADING FROM THE MIDDLE

What if you are a church leader but not the primary ordained leader of the congregation, such as the rector or pastor? The same principles apply to lay leaders, assisting clergy, and members of the church staff, in slightly different ways. Your relationships are just as critical. If you are leading a ministry area, work on developing key relationships with others in that ministry area. If you have a boss, work on that relationship as diligently as you can.

Is it harder to be the leader at the top or a leader in the middle? Both types of leaders have different and equally difficult challenges. Top leaders get more recognition (both praise and blame), usually more rewards (financial and otherwise), yet also carry more of the burden. Leaders in the middle have to chart their leadership course based on the direction from above, which can be an arduous task. Sometimes they have more freedom, sometimes less, depending on the type of pastor or rector, but they usually carry less of the overall burden.

The basic principles of leadership remain the same in a middle position: be as clear as you can be about your own purpose and direction, and stay connected to those around you, both above and below. Of course, there are differences in the way we relate to those above us than to those we lead directly. A rector or senior pastor has authority, and charts the overall course. It is worth learning as much as you can about your immediate boss or supervisor and other top leaders: be curious about their life experiences, and watch how they function in the system of which you are all a part. Become a researcher in your church, and you will be less anxious and better prepared to face the inevitable ups and downs. You will also be better off if you are as clear as possible about what your job is and what it is not, and who you are responsible to. Many churches are not very clear on this, even for paid staff.

Dr. Robert Dibble, long-time Minister to Adults at River Road Church (Baptist) in Richmond, Virginia, describes his experiences in navigating the change of senior pastors after fifteen years and not connecting early enough with the new pastor. After a difficult transition, he says, "I decided that I would work on coming to him and keeping him informed, being more proactive about expressing my opinion. If I'm silent about matters that I'm concerned about, then I've abdicated my authority." It is often possible to lead by maintaining this kind of intentional connection, and have an influence on the top leader's direction by the nature of our presence, particularly if the top leader is open to that connection.

We can also work on some clarity about our own bottom line—what we will and will not put up with. For those in the middle, this is particularly important if the top leader either wants peace at any price or is a hostile force. The conflict-avoidant leader may be just as dangerous as the unpredictable and autocratic one. Here, having a bottom line, clear boundaries, and multiple options is critical. Thinking through options and having an exit strategy—whether we use it or not—can be useful for any leader, and can free us up for more creative thinking about the challenges at hand. If we feel like we have to stay, we will feel stuck and find it harder to be flexible and imaginative. If we see options, we will feel freer and be better able to make a contribution to our own area of ministry and to the whole life of the parish.

☙ THE RELAY RACE OF LEADERSHIP

We are also in relationship with those leaders who have gone before, and those who will come after us. The author of the letter to the Hebrews refers to the great "cloud of witnesses" that surrounds us as we "run with perseverance the race that is set before us" (12:1). Keeping that fact in mind can help us maintain perspective on the progress we have made. If we feel we are lagging behind, perhaps it is because we are facing challenges bequeathed to us by our predecessors. If we feel we are doing well, it is in part due to the strengths of those who went before. If we are starting something entirely new, we can remember our hopes for those who come after, and start thinking about the future and planning for succession.

As in a relay race, the leadership handoff is important. Transitions from one leader to another are key times for any institution. When we are leaving, we can be aware of our own vulnerability to loss and transition—wanting to hang on too long, or wanting to get out as quickly as possible, or wanting to make our mark as soon as possible.

Entering a new system requires the same rigorous attention. Ed Bacon describes the way he tried to enter his new
congregation as a researcher. He followed a popular twenty-
eight-year rector, and had made a major move himself, so he
knew everyone's anxiety would be high. He realized he had
a lot to learn about the parish, both where they had been and
where they wanted to go. He believed he would serve them
better if he stayed in "research mode," approaching the parish
as a learner rather than an expert. So he took a legal pad to
every single meeting he attended, and took notes. Thirteen
years later, people still refer back to his legal pads, remembering the way he was really interested in learning about
them. Now, beginning a major capital campaign, he says, "I'm
trying to schedule meetings to stay connected, and trying to
be the listener." The need to connect intentionally lasts
through a ministry, from beginning to end.

We make more progress when we focus on our own functioning, without blaming others who have gone before us or
feeling like we must measure up to a glorious past. Our task
is to pay attention to our own part in the story right now. We
should not get distracted from the steps we need to take
today.

This does not mean we ignore those who have gone
before. We can look for times to invite living predecessors
back to connect the institution with the ongoing race. We
can ask about stories that need to be told, to give ourselves
and others energy to keep persevering. Obstacles overcome
in the past may inspire us in the present.

When my iconic predecessor, the Reverend Ruth
Thompson, died about ten years into my ministry, the church
held a memorial service at the family's request. She had been
retired for over twenty years, after a twenty-one-year ministry
in that congregation. Church members as well as family
members had the opportunity to tell stories about her ministry, and I had the chance to overhear them. I felt more
deeply connected to the congregation. After that we all found

energy for new initiatives: in particular, a local mission effort and increased pastoral care training for our deacons.

The story does not end with us. Occasionally reminding ourselves and everyone else that our tenure is not forever can help those we lead to dream big about the future, and to become less dependent on our leadership. And it can help us keep perspective on the place of our own leadership in the whole story of the congregation's ministry.

❧ QUESTIONS TO PONDER

Church leadership is about relationships: not just taking care of people in pastoral care, but developing relationships in the interest of leadership goals. This is not a self-serving endeavor, but one which benefits everyone, as we all move forward together. Connection with our congregation is an act of spiritual leadership. True connection with another human being means we honor who that person is: a child of God, created and gifted. We approach other people with respect, recognizing both their gifts and their potential, and the possibilities for what we can all do together.

Here are four questions to ask yourself when thinking about the importance of relationships in your ministry and congregation:

- ✍ Who are the key leaders in my church and how am I connecting with them? How often?

- ✍ How do I tend to respond when things get anxious: do I aggressively engage, withdraw, or do something else? How could I try another way to relate when conflicts arise?

- ✍ What did I learn about relationships from my family? How are those strengths and weaknesses showing up in my ministry?

- ✍ How am I relating to those above me in the congregational or denominational structure?

CHAPTER 10

SAY YOUR
PRAYERS

On a recent trip to Colorado I was advised to drink a lot of water to help prevent altitude sickness. Whenever I forgot this advice, I became dizzy and began to get a headache; drinking a big glass of water made me feel better almost instantly. As church leaders, we also attempt to reach challenging heights. And just as I needed to drink plenty of water for my body to work well at Colorado mountain altitudes, if we do not take in enough spiritual nourishment, we will not function well as church leaders. We will get dizzy and lose our balance as a leader. Some leaders do stumble and fall—physically, emotionally, or morally. Yet we can choose to seek out resources that can sustain us, so we do not find ourselves spiritually ill and unable to go on.

"Drinking in" spiritual nourishment on a regular basis involves more than going to conferences to learn the latest ministry technique or even studying the Bible to prepare for sermons. We need the resources of Scripture, prayer, and worship for our own sake, not simply for Sunday. We need spiritual practices that go beyond our profession; if we do not have this kind of sustenance, over time we will wear out from the ongoing ministry challenges. Yes, we have to work on relationships in the congregation, but we must also pay attention to our relationship with God if we are to have anything to give to others.

As we learn who we are at the deepest level through regular spiritual practice, we will be ourselves and communicate our authenticity. God has made and gifted each of us uniquely: this is the most important spiritual aspect of leadership. The better we know ourselves, and live that out in our leadership role, the more we can sustain ourselves through the inevitable ups and downs of ministry. It may seem simpler to search for a formula for leadership, but we will need less energy to be ourselves and to lead as God made us if we stop trying to imitate others. Just as it is more comfortable to wear clothes that fit rather than squeeze into something too small or flounder in something too large, when we try to use a preprogrammed approach to leadership, other people will know we are wearing someone else's costume.

In the story told in 1 Samuel 17 of David fighting the giant Goliath, David rejects the heavy armor that King Saul tries to give him. "I cannot walk with these," he says. He knows how he works best. He takes the armor off and confronts Goliath in the way he knows best, with stones and a slingshot. Like David, when we know who we are, we will be more at home in our role. We will be better prepared to face the challenges of ministry when we adopt and develop spiritual practices that are right for us.

❧ MEDITATION AND LEADERSHIP

Some years into my ministry, I attended a retreat on spirituality led by Joan Hickey of the Shalem Institute in Washington, D.C. She assigned us a meditation exercise using the words of Jesus to his disciples: "Who do you say I am?" (Matthew 16:15). She suggested that we ask Jesus that question in prayer, about ourselves—asking Jesus imaginatively, "Who do *you* say *I* am?" I took that exercise away with me and used it over and over in the weeks to come. And I began practicing meditative prayer for the first time in my life. I found, and still find, that I never do it "well" (a good lesson for a perfectionist), but it benefits my life and leadership. It helps me know who I am and what God calls me to be and do.

Why practice meditation? It is one way to follow Jesus' admonition to take the log out of our own eye first. In meditation we pay attention to ourselves. To begin with, you simply have to sit still, a good discipline for leaders who find themselves in the sometimes frantic world of pastoral leadership. For goal-oriented leaders, it is hard to feel like we are doing anything when we are meditating, yet in fact meditation can actually benefit our leadership. Practiced over time, we can find ourselves better able to wait, to listen, and to be present with people. And we can make decisions and move forward with a greater sense of calm and less anxiety. These qualities can benefit our leadership. Meditation is not magic; it requires a real investment of ourselves in the practice. And it is not quick—this is not "thirty days of meditation to a new you." The real impact of the practice comes over years, not days.

Those who practice meditation consistently find themselves less reactive, with a greater range of choices in their response to others. A Zen story illustrates this spiritual steadiness. The students in the monastery were in awe of the elder monk, not because he was strict, but because nothing ever seemed to upset or ruffle him. Indeed, they found him a bit unearthly and even frightening. One day they decided to put him to a test. A group of them very quietly hid in a dark corner of a hallway and waited for the monk to walk by. Within moments, the old man appeared, carrying a cup of hot tea. Just as he passed by, the students all rushed out at him, screaming as loud as they could. But the monk showed no reaction whatsoever. He peacefully made his way to a small table at the end of the hall, gently placed the cup down, and then, leaning against the wall, cried out with shock.[27]

What if we could have that kind of self-management when someone criticizes our sermon at the door, or acts up in a council meeting? It would be worth giving something up to spend time in meditation. For most of us, to be able to manage our response in the face of an emotional ambush is a distant dream, but we all can get better at it. When we regularly engage in the practice of sitting quietly in meditation over months and years, we learn to deal with our own anxiety. Meditation, when practiced as a process of growth and not merely a technique, can help us learn to experience anxiety without reacting. It helps us be in the moment.

ཙ LEADERSHIP IN THE MOMENT

Another practice that can help leadership is simple awareness, in the midst of our work and the rest of our life. A specific meditation or retreat time is not the only opportunity to do this work. We can practice being aware of God's presence through the day. We can focus on spiritual growth and on this moment even amid the stresses of daily work. And this practice actually takes no extra time.

Even so, God's call to live in the moment challenges us, especially when we are always thinking about next Sunday, the next stewardship campaign, the next church we hope to serve. Or we are thinking about last Sunday's sermon, that last council meeting, the last budget deficit. Yet what lies directly in front of us is *this* conversation with my spouse, *this* prayer I am offering right now, *this* sunshine coming in the window. As we bring this awareness to each moment, we become less frantic and more present with each person. Living in the moment does not mean we live only for self-indulgence, or never work on healing past wounds, or never make plans for the future. Still, we acknowledge that the only moment we have any power over is the one we are living right now. Today, this minute, I can choose to act with love, with grace, to be present to those I am with, whether my child, a church member, or a stranger.

The goal, as Teresa of Avila noted, is to be Mary and Martha at the same time. Mary sat at Jesus' feet and learned;

Martha worked serving the meal. Teresa suggested that the ideal was to be serving and sitting at Jesus' feet at the same time. So in the middle of the busyness, we are in Christ's presence. We can be conscious of God's presence as we work. Our other prayer practices help us do this, but we also need to pay attention through the day, to keep bringing our awareness back to God again and again.

Rowan Williams, the Archbishop of Canterbury, is no stranger to the challenges of leadership. He writes this about conscious spiritual awareness in the midst of the busyness of work:

> I have signed the fifteenth letter of the morning and made the fourth uncomfortable phone call. I have emerged from a meeting about next year's budget, and I am getting ready for a session with our investment advisors after lunch. After which I have to go and take an afternoon's school assembly. Probably in the evening, I'll have to institute a new parish priest somewhere. All of it is all right. All of it has also got to be done. But I think, "Was it all for this?" The only thing I find that helps is to let myself be simply drawn into the present moment. This means making a point sometimes of looking at what is on this side of the window pane in the office or putting my hands on the arms of a chair and feeling the fabric. And breathing, saying, "Well, here I am. This is what I must do next; the basket-weaving stuff.".... All I can do here and now is to say, "God is in this moment."[28]

God is in every moment of our life in ministry, if we only can know it. When we stop, even for a breath, and remember it, we will be better able to get through this meeting, that difficult conversation, tomorrow's long day. And we will show up with more energy and presence.

❧ LEADERSHIP AND SILENCE

A third spiritual practice is that of silence. Leaders need silence. Most of us are not quiet; we thrive on the busyness, the demands, and the contact with people. But leading requires clear thinking, which requires silence and solitude to develop. When an elderly parishioner got a hearing aid, she pronounced to me, "It's a noisy, noisy world!" The constant noise of radio, television, and cell phones becomes static, interfering with our own thinking. Rarely do we find silence. Even when the office is quiet, the computers are still humming. The noise of a city surrounds many of us. The barrage of input wears us down.

During a visit to a Trappist monastery, I spent nearly twenty-four hours in silence. I expected the time to drag; instead, I was amazed when I looked at my watch to find the day was almost over. The enforced silence was wonderful, a bit to my surprise. Even the silent meals, initially awkward, became a gift, as the need to fill the air with conversation was taken away. I hiked alone to the top of a hill that was steeper than I thought I could manage. I noticed nature in a new way. I found myself thinking new thoughts about the world and my place in it.

Silence as a spiritual practice means we find ways to shut out the noise. We create times when we are not available to others. We put away the iPod and turn off the cell phone. We may be able to create silent space at church, or we may have to go elsewhere. We can do any number of things in silent space: sit and meditate, pray, read or write, walk, even jog. But we need to hush the insistent audio input that is always present in our society. And checking e-mail and surfing the Internet do not count, even in a silent room!

The best leaders know what they think and believe, know their deepest convictions in life. This takes silence. Ultimately, we have to face ourselves and be alone in order to figure out what we think. When we have that kind of clarity about life, we can go on for a long time. We have inner reserves that will not be depleted by the relentless demands of leadership, of those who want our ear and want their way, of those who act out and act up, and of our constantly changing environment. While facing these demands is never easy, we can build up our reserves through ongoing attention to our own spiritual growth.

The Reverend Jeffery Savage, pastor of First Baptist Church in Springfield, Oregon, emphasizes the *practicality* of silence: "The practical implications of learning to be quiet are that you can come back and be slow to speak and slow to anger: that I can learn to control my mouth. We use words to manage and control people's impressions of us, to manipulate, to get people to do what we want. To stop talking removes us from that endless loop of doing that, to rely on God rather than on our own ability to manage it."

In most ministry settings outside a monastery, silence is not built in. We have to make it happen. We have to schedule it for five minutes today, an hour next week, a retreat next month. If silence is difficult for you, start small. Start with five minutes, and turn off your cell phone while you do it. You may find over time that instead of dreading silence, you look forward to it.

✎ PRAYING FOR OTHERS

Praying for those we lead and others in need is another practice that is worth cultivating. In my Baptist tradition, we often say, "I'll pray for you," or someone will say, "Pray for me," but I wonder how often most of us make good on that promise. When we do pray for others, we tend to make elaborate requests of God and offer detailed lists of how we want God to handle the situation. I have found that having a regular routine of simply mentioning the names of key people in prayer helps me actually practice intercessory prayer. It also keeps me from overfunctioning with God by saying what I think God should do.

The Reverend Todd Miller, rector of Trinity Episcopal Parish in Newton Centre, Massachusetts, takes his church directory to noonday prayer and prays his way through it regularly, one page a day. "I'm beginning to think that my primary role as their priest is to pray for them," Miller says. "It keeps my parishioners, all of them, on my screen." In a practice like this, you cannot skip over the difficult people. They all regularly come through the cycle.

When we pray for those in our congregation, it changes our relationship with them. We are in fact creating a triangle with God when we pray, allowing God to take on some of our anxiety for those we are praying for. This can allow us to be calmer in our relationship with those with whom we may have difficulty. It can also allow us to get some distance from those we are very close to who may be struggling with life, offering them to God rather than jumping in to help or fix. Over time, we will often see a significant shift in how we relate to others when we pray for them regularly. The purpose of this kind of prayer is really to change *us,* rather than asking God to change *them.*

❧ OUR OWN FAITH STORY

One often hidden dimension of our spirituality is the way we relate to the tradition we grew up in. We do not usually think about this as a spiritual practice, but when we bring spiritual awareness to our faith heritage, it will help us with our leadership. Whether we remained with that tradition or have chosen another, have we achieved some perspective on it? If so, we will be better spiritual leaders.

Whether we are too slavishly attached to our inherited religious heritage or have rejected it too thoughtlessly, it can trip us up in ministry. This can be just as true of a family tradition of militant atheism as of religious fundamentalism. Working on developing perspective in relation to our faith tradition challenges us to think through our own principles and beliefs, and can help us relate with more flexibility toward the tradition. This practice can help us develop our own spiritual maturity.

We can explore this in several ways. First, we can reflect on our own faith journey and that of our family. Second, we can pray for our family just as we pray for our congregation. Finally, we can learn more about how our family came to have the faith (or mixture of faiths) they had.

As we explore our family faith story, we may be surprised by what we find. One minister who thought she had no one of faith in her family story remembered a close friend of the family who was like an uncle to her. When some of his fishing buddies said, "We looked all over hell for you!" she remembered him saying, "Well, you were looking in the wrong place!" She had forgotten that she had a person of faith in her early life, and that her subsequent journey into ministry did not come out of nowhere. In another case, a Baptist pastor who thought he was the first person in his family to choose that tradition discovered his great-grandfather had founded the first Baptist church in western Kansas. His Baptist roots actually went deep into the past. If you chose a different tradition, keep your eyes open for what you may find in generations past. Your own family may surprise you.

In my own case, I grew up in a Protestant evangelical family. The day I was born, my father left the hospital to go to the train station to pick up a missionary who was to speak at our church that night. He handed out candy rather than cigars to everyone at the station, announcing "It's a girl!" I first went to church when I was three weeks old. My mother's father was a pastor, and his father used to visit the original Pentecostal revival meetings on Azusa Street in Los Angeles. The church forms an integral part of my family multigenerational process.

One of the efforts I made to "define yourself in the place that defined you," as Larry Matthews puts it, was a visit with my parents to an anniversary celebration for the evangelical church we attended for about ten years when I was young. I saw people who had known me since I was six years old, experienced their delight at our visit, and reconnected with people I had attended youth group with. During the anniversary service they invited all the pastors and former pastors, elders and former elders, deacons and former deacons to come forward and stand on the steps in front. As I watched the array of leaders in front, which included my own father, I noticed there were about fifty of them—all men. For a moment I felt wounded as I saw them, and as I remembered my experience growing up as a girl in that church. Some of the boys had been tapped on the shoulder and invited to consider ministry, but I had not been.

Then I paused, and realized that before me lay a spiritual choice: I could choose whether or not to be wounded by this experience, past and present. I may be a better minister because of the challenges I faced as a girl and a woman, as I tried to find my place in leadership in the church. I had to find a church that would ordain me and allow me to serve as a pastoral leader, unlike the churches I grew up in. Even within the denomination I chose, I struggled to find a church to call me, and moved across the country to take that call. Perhaps I can function outside the church structures in my current ministry because of that position on the outside early in life.

When we came out of the service of celebration, my father said, "You know, if we still lived here, I'd still like to attend this church!" Instantly, I felt betrayed. I could feel my heart begin to pound. I was immediately caught up in reactivity, and said defensively, "Would you really want to attend a church where they didn't allow women to be leaders?"

"No, no, of course not!" he responded. But I still felt outraged. I had to go through the drill again, noticing my physical and emotional reaction and breathing until I calmed down. Later I could laugh at myself that I got so easily hooked—and I have had plenty of opportunities since. Every conversation with my parents about church, every week as I attend worship, every encounter with the clergy and church leaders I coach and consult with provides another chance to practice.

Many clergy leaders are surprised to discover other ministers in generations past that they never knew about—the opposite of a skeleton in the family closet. Others find a greater sense of connection with their own family, and a deeper claiming of their own call to ministry. Bringing a new awareness to your family experience and getting curious about your family's life of faith can help you find out more about who you are.

ᕯ FINDING TIME FOR SPIRITUAL GROWTH

The practices described here are not the only ones that can help sustain us spiritually. Here are some other ways we can work on our spiritual growth:

Worship in different places and traditions.
Find a place to worship where you are not in charge and attend services at least quarterly.

Go outside.
Find a tree and lean against it, and recognize the God-given strength that comes from the earth. This strength is also available to you as a leader.

Find a spiritual mentor.
Finding a wise leader or a spiritual director who is grounded spiritually, with whom you can meet regularly to discuss your spiritual life and practice, will encourage your growth.

Read Scripture devotionally, not just for your sermon preparation.
Meditating on one verse a day is better than none, and it may be better than a whole chapter. We need to encounter the Scriptures in ways not related to our own productivity.

Try some new practice or discipline.
If you are inclined to contemplative prayer or if your tradition uses only informal prayers, try using written prayers. If you always use written prayers, practice pouring your heart out to God. If you love silence, join a prayer group. This is about developing your spiritual repertoire.

To carry out most of these practices, setting aside a regular time for quiet and prayer is important. Clergy find it easy to be caught up in the relentless demands of others. I often ask the clergy I work with about their spiritual practice or prayer life. The answer frequently is, "Well, I know I should...," or, "I should do more...." Prayer can become simply one more undone item on the endless to-do list. Yet even a moment of stopping in the flow of relentless activity can bring a shift in perspective—no small gift.

Finding time for prayer can be a constant struggle. It can also be a decision. I need to eat every day, so I do. I need to pray every day, so I do. No question. Now, some days I have to grab a quick lunch. Some days, I may only have five minutes for prayer. Five minutes are not enough on a regular basis, but five minutes are better than no minutes.

"Pray without ceasing," Paul says (1 Thessalonians 5:17). You can pray in the midst of your ministry, but sustained pastoral ministry means finding some sustained time for prayer. Rather than "I ought to pray more," another approach might be, "Prayer will help me with my ministry more than anything else I can do."

⮞ FINDING OUR TRUEST SELF
None of these practices is an end in itself. Their purpose is to help us learn who we are, to find our truest self. As we discover who God made us to be, we can sustain ourselves through the roller-coaster ride of leadership, better able to keep our sense of balance and our sense of humor. We will be

less dependent on what other people think of us and better able to live out of our deepest convictions and purpose.

In ministry, as in the rest of life, it is all too easy to live out of what Thomas Merton called the "false self":

> If I do not know who I am, it is because I think I am the sort of person everyone around me wants to be. Perhaps I have never asked myself whether I really wanted to become what everybody else seems to want to become. Perhaps if I only realized that I do not admire what everyone seems to admire, I would really begin to live after all.

Merton contrasted the false self with the true self. He said this of the true self:

> For me to be a saint means to be myself. Therefore the problem of sanctity and salvation is in fact the problem of finding out who I am and of discovering my true self.[29]

We all live out of the false or pseudo-self, at least some of the time. We are all dependent to some degree on the response of others. In a similar vein, Murray Bowen taught about the "solid self" and the "pseudo-self":

> The solid self says, "This is who I am, what I believe, what I stand for, and what I will do or will not do," in a given situation. The solid self is made up of clearly defined beliefs, opinions, convictions, and life principles. . . . The pseudo-self is composed of a vast assortment of principles, beliefs, philosophies, and knowledge acquired because it is required or considered right by the group.[30]

Our many roles can function this way. Roles are essential in life, for us and for those who relate to us. But we can easily depend on the role of "pastor" or "deacon" or "senior warden" or "Sunday school teacher." I worked for many years to be less dependent on my role as pastor of a church, but when I eventually left that role, I was astonished by how lost I felt. I would go to church every Sunday and sit in a pew and surreptitiously dab the tears from the corners of my eyes as I watched the service proceed. I had chosen to leave the pastorate to develop a new ministry. But who was I without the role of "pastor"?

Only God can tell us who we truly are, so we need to develop ways to encounter God apart from the role. In the busyness and stress of ministry, it is astonishingly easy to avoid this encounter. And over time, that avoidance takes its toll. We lead more and more out of the false self, and our true self takes a back seat, to the detriment of ourselves, those we love, and our ministry. Paradoxically, when we are less attached to our role and less needy of the approval and acceptance of others, we are better able to bring our whole and truest self to our ministry. As the thirteenth-century mystic Mechtild of Magdeburg wrote:

> Each creature God made
> Must live in its own true nature;
> How could I resist my nature,
> That lives for oneness with God?[31]

❧ PATIENCE AND PERSISTENCE

My grandfather served as a Baptist pastor from 1920 to 1970, in a world that was very different from ours, with an approach to his Christian faith and ministry that is very different from mine. Yet as I think back over my memories of him, I see aspects of his approach to leadership that I use myself. He was in active ministry for most of those fifty years, and came out of retirement twice. He worked hard, yet he made room for family in his ministry. My mother remembers that she never felt like she was interrupting him, even when his office was at home. He faced setbacks and kept going, recovering from more than one experience where he was forced out of a position. He was able to be flexible and adapt over time, while staying true to his principles. Mom remembers him saying, "Don't be the first one in or the last one out." He remained conservative to the end. Still, he was, on balance, open to new things. I was ordained when he was ninety-one, and he wrote me a letter that said, "Your grandmother and I don't exactly know about women in ministry, but we pray for you every day."

We receive some gifts for ministry from our family heritage, along with the booby traps. These are a few of the gifts I've received: perseverance, commitment to family, openness. What strengths has your family given you for your work? For some families, simply surviving can be a strength. Whether or not your family was involved in church and ministry, they gave you some gifts which you use every day. What are they?

Laurence Gonzales writes about survivors, and his first "rule of life" is, "Be here now." "It's a good survival rule," he says. "It means to pay attention and keep an up-to-date mental model."[32] In other words, look at reality and not at what you *think* reality is. We can look at the real situation in our church and our ministry without pretending things are better than they are, and without simply bemoaning the challenges. We simply bring our best thinking to the reality of the moment.

The second rule is this: "Everything takes eight times as long as it's supposed to." So as we persevere, we can recognize this reality. The stories of miraculous results, whether in the church or elsewhere, leave out the first seven parts of the effort. There are few if any overnight successes, but persistence and perseverance pay off. As I noted earlier, it may take five years before a pastor can truly articulate a vision for a congregation.

Bringing yourself to your ministry is fundamental to lasting leadership. As I have said, working on your own growth is the best gift you can give to those you lead. We have seen some ways to do that, through taking responsibility for ourselves, noticing triangles, learning our own family story, and clarifying our own purpose every day as well as in times of crisis.

The second letter to Timothy speaks of "a spirit of power and of love and of self-discipline" (1:7). When we lead from these qualities, we are able to be present in the moment, in love for God and those we lead. God gives us a spirit of power—the power of the Holy Spirit, available for ministry to all Christians, ordained or lay. God gives us a spirit of love, which helps us put in the time on the clock and on the calendar we need to build relationships that can make real ministry happen. Finally, God gives us a spirit of self-discipline— what Edwin Friedman called "self-regulation."

This spirit helps us learn to respond, and not merely react. We can take a deep breath and step back, recognizing that the leader needs to keep the big picture and not merely get caught up in the moment. We can be disciplined enough to make difficult decisions even if we would rather avoid or procrastinate. We can stay longer, rather than resign quickly. And, most difficult of all, we can act, even in the face of uncertainty and criticism. As the late Krister Stendahl suggested, "Doing something for the Lord is a safe way to humility, for others will cut you down. There is no absolute clarity—except for fundamentalists. You are never sure in the ultimate sense whether your decisions are right or wrong. God is the ultimate judge."[33] We can be disciplined enough to make the big and difficult decisions, even if we are not sure of the outcome.

QUESTIONS TO PONDER
Leadership is sustainable. But it requires the qualities of spirit that are bestowed on us as a gift of God. We are given the Spirit of God, along with the life force given us at creation. We have a powerful connection with God, which we can develop and encourage by the regular practice of prayer and worship. As we engage in these practices, we will find it easier to discern our own leadership direction and calling. In

the end, the gift that we bring to our ministry, whether it is congregational leadership or elsewhere, lay or ordained, is the gift of ourselves. The more we tap into our own unique gift, the more we rekindle the fire that God lit in us at the time of our calling, the fire that is unlike anyone else.

Here are some final questions for you to consider as you continue your own ministry:

- What is the unique power that God has given me?

- What are the bottom-line values and principles that are most important to me?

- Who are the people in my ministry setting that I most need to work on relating to with love?

- Who in my family do I need to relate to with love?

- Where do I need to exercise some self-discipline or self-regulation? Some moderation?

- What are some specific ways I can put this discipline into practice? Getting up in the morning for prayer? Taking a day off? Keeping my cool at a council or vestry meeting? Saying no to someone?

As we learn to understand the forces that shaped us, the vision that compels us, and the people who make our leadership possible, we will be better able to know where to go and how to get there. Leadership does not happen overnight, and it does not happen in a vacuum. If we are in it for the long term, so much the better. As we face the challenges of sustaining our leadership over time, we are not alone. Leadership can be a lonely path, as I am sure Paul knew well. But the Holy Spirit is within us to sustain us and renew us, if we take the time to rekindle or stir the coals. "Stir up the gift that is within you" (2 Timothy 1:6). This is not a one-time effort, but a lifetime of remembering our story and the church's story as we continue to receive the gift of being leaders in Christ's church.

ENDNOTES

1. Wallace Stegner, *Wolf Willow* (New York: Penguin Books, 2000), 217, 219.

2. Joan Chittister, *The Rule of Benedict: Insights for the Ages* (New York: Crossroad, 1992), 38.

3. Gerald May, "Don't Be a Pest," *Shalem News* (Summer 1997).

4. "A History of the Diocese of Newark," Diocese of Newark Profile Committee, 2005.

5. Ronald W. Richardson, *Becoming a Healthier Pastor* (Minneapolis: Fortress Press, 2005), 61.

6. Two resources are Israel Galindo, Elaine Boomer, and Don Reagan, *The Family Genogram Workbook* (Richmond: Educational Consultants, 2006) and Ronald W. Richardson, *Family Ties That Bind* (Bellingham: Self-Counsel, 1995).

7. For more on triangles, see Edwin H. Friedman, *A Failure of Nerve* (New York: Seabury Books, 2007), 204–228. For a comprehensive look at triangles, see Peter Titelman, ed., *Triangles: Bowen Family Systems Theory Perspective* (New York: Haworth, 2008).

8. Titelman, *Triangles,* 43.

9. Ernest Kurtz and Katherine Ketcham, *The Spirituality of Imperfection: Storytelling and the Search for Meaning* (New York: Bantam Books, 1993), 91.

10. Jerry Kramer, ed., *Lombardi: Winning Is the Only Thing* (New York: Thomas Y. Crowell Co., 1976), 251.

11. *Tao Te Ching,* trans. Stephen Mitchell (New York: Harper & Row, 1988), 15.

12. Edwin Friedman, *The Myth of the Shiksa* (New York: Seabury Books, 2008), 158.

13. Parker Palmer, *Let Your Life Speak: Listening for the Voice of Vocation* (San Francisco: Jossey-Bass, 1999), 10.

14. *Tao Te Ching,* 10.

15. Lawrence E. Matthews, "Leadership: Viewed through a Family Systems Lens"; http://www.leadershipinministry.com/leadership_through_self-di.htm.

16. Friedman, *A Failure of Nerve,* 174.

17. Israel Galindo, *The Hidden Lives of Congregations* (Herndon, Va: The Alban Institute, 2004), 143.

18. See Christine Wicker, *The Fall of the Evangelical Nation: The Surprising Crisis Inside the Church* (New York: HarperOne, 2008).

19. E. F. Schumacher, *Small Is Beautiful: Economics as if People Mattered* (New York: HarperPerennial, 1989), 102–104.

20. Dean R. Hoge and Jacqueline E. Wenger, *Pastors in Transition: Why Clergy Leave Local Church Ministry* (Grand Rapids: Eerdmans, 2005), 171.

21. My sources for the Shackleton story include Caroline Alexander, *The Endurance: Shackleton's Legendary Antarctic Expedition* (New York: Knopf, 1998) and Alfred Lansing, *Endurance: Shackleton's Incredible Voyage* (New York: McGraw-Hill, 1959).

22. Quoted in Alexander, *Endurance,* 44.

23. See chapter eight of Friedman's *A Failure of Nerve* for much more on the crucial topic of sabotage.

24. Alexander, *Endurance,* 161.

25. Alexander, *Endurance,* 66.

26. Margaret B. Hess, "High Anxiety," *The Christian Century* (July 15, 2008): 12–13.

27. "Surprising the Master," in *Zen Stories to Tell Your Neighbors;* http://www-usr.rider.edu/~suler/zenstory/surprise.html.

28. Rowan Williams, *Where God Happens* (Boston: New Seeds, 2005), 96–97.

29. Thomas Merton, *Seeds,* ed. Robert Inchausti (Boston: Shambhala, 2002), 4, 155.

30. Murray Bowen, *Family Therapy in Clinical Practice* (New York: Aronson, 1978), 365.

31. Mechtild of Magdeburg, "A fish cannot drown in water," trans. Jane Hirshfield, *The Enlightened Heart,* ed. Stephen Mitchell (New York: HarperPerennial, 1993), 64.

32. Laurence Gonzales, *Deep Survival* (New York: Norton, 2003), 127.

33. Yehezkel Landau, "An Interview with Krister Stendahl," *Harvard Divinity Bulletin* (Winter 2007): 30–31.

RESOURCES

BOOKS

Friedman, Edwin H. *A Failure of Nerve*. New York: Seabury Books, 2007.

Friedman, Edwin H. *Generation to Generation: Family Process in Church and Synagogue*. New York: Guilford, 1985.

Friedman, Edwin H. *The Myth of the Shiksa*. New York: Seabury Books, 2008.

Galindo, Israel, Elaine Boomer, and Don Reagan. *The Family Genogram Workbook*. Richmond: Educational Consultants, 2006.

Galindo, Israel. *The Hidden Lives of Congregations: Discerning Church Dynamics*. Herndon, Va.: The Alban Institute, 2004.

Gilbert, Roberta M. *Extraordinary Relationships*. Minneapolis: Chronimed, 1992.

Hoge, Dean R., and Jacqueline E. Wenger. *Pastors in Transition: Why Clergy Leave Local Church Ministry*. Grand Rapids: Eerdmans, 2005.

Kurtz, Ernest, and Katherine Ketcham. *The Spirituality of Imperfection: Storytelling and the Search for Meaning.* New York: Bantam Books, 1993.

Richardson, Ronald W. *Becoming a Healthier Pastor: Family Systems Theory and the Pastor's Own Family.* Minneapolis: Fortress Press, 2005.

Richardson, Ronald W. *Creating a Healthier Church: Family Systems Theory, Leadership, and Congregational Life.* Minneapolis: Fortress Press, 1996.

Richardson, Ronald W. *Family Ties That Bind.* Bellingham: Self-Counsel, 1995.

Steinke. Peter L. *Congregational Leadership in Anxious Times: Being Calm and Courageous No Matter What.* Herndon, Va.: The Alban Institute, 2006.

Titelman, Peter, ed. *Triangles: Bowen Family Systems Theory Perspective.* New York: Haworth, 2008.

AUDIO / VIDEO RESOURCES

Friedman, Edwin H. *Family Process and Process Theology.* Herndon, Va: The Alban Institute, 1991. (DVD)

Friedman, Edwin H. "A Failure of Nerve: Leadership in the Age of the Quick Fix." (Set of four lectures given in 1996; available from Russell Martin, P.O. Box 858, Painesville, OH 44077; revm44@ameritech.net.)

WEBSITES AND BLOGS

Bowen Center for the Study of the Family
www.thebowencenter.org
Information about Bowen family systems theory; books, audio and video resources available for purchase.

G.R.A.C.E. Writes
grace-ed.org/blog
Israel Galindo writes regularly on a wide variety of topics for this blog.

Ideas to Action
ideastoaction.wordpress.com
Andrea Maloney-Schara worked closely with Murray Bowen, and is working to apply his ideas to leadership in society.

Leadership in Ministry
www.leadershipinministry.com.
Articles, newsletter, and training programs for clergy.

Margaret Marcuson
www.margaretmarcuson.com
My own website and blog describe my latest thinking about leadership and ministry.

Western Pennsylvania Family Center
www.wpfc.net
Offers many videos by Murray Bowen and a number by Edwin Friedman, available for borrowing by members.